SERIES TWO

INTERMEDIATE
BRIDGE

I LOVE BRIDGE
THE VALENTINE SERIES

SERIES ONE   BEGINNER/REFRESHER BRIDGE

SERIES TWO   INTERMEDIATE BRIDGE

SERIES THREE   ADVANCED BRIDGE

To purchase any of the above books in the series,
visit our website at www.ilovebridgebooks.com

Special thanks to Barry Rigal for his insights and editing skills. Mr. Rigal holds title to two North American Bridge Championships, is a bridge commenter and journalist, and co-editor of the American Contract Bridge League's *Encyclopedia of Bridge.*

Also, thanks to editors Sandy Forsythe and Richard Pavlicek, and to my students for their support in developing the material for the books during our many bridge classes.

Table of Contents   Look for the ⬡ to show important text.

THE HISTORY OF BRIDGE

The origin of playing cards and China's invention of paper dates back to the year 979 A.D. Card games such as triumph and ruff and honors were played primarily in England in the 16th century, and these games evolved into the card game "whist". Whist was made famous by Edmond Hoyle's book, *"A Short Treatise on the Game of Whist,"* published in 1742.

Whist was introduced to the United States in 1690, and went through many stages of evolution in the following centuries. George Washington enjoyed playing whist and placed small wagers on the game.

The English began playing duplicate whist in 1857. Duplicate play was introduced to eliminate the luck of the deal, as players could play the same hands and compare scores. Duplicate whist was introduced to the United States in 1880, and Americans began playing in duplicate club matches in 1883.

The game of bridge evolved from whist. Early documentation notes that the name bridge may have derived from the Russian term "Biritch" which means players announce or herald their auction. In 1890, bridge replaced whist in England and in the United States.

Harold S. Vanderbilt created a new method of scoring while playing bridge on a cruise with friends and family through the Panama Canal in 1925. Thus, contract bridge was born.

Ely Culbertson published his best-selling books, *"The Culbertson Summary"* and the *"Blue Book,"* in 1931. In 1958, Charles Goren appeared on the cover of Time Magazine, and was named "The King of Aces." The Time article proclaimed bridge as the worlds number one card game.

Bill Gates, Warren Buffet, Omar Sharif and Catherine Zeta Jones are some of the many celebrities playing bridge today. President Eisenhower played bridge regularly with top experts and attended national bridge tournaments.

Bridge is considered an important exercise in maintaining intellectual alertness. The game is stimulating, competitive, and socially rewarding. Experienced players are continually learning new concepts, and there are thousands of books written on the subject of the game. Today, bridge is played and enjoyed by many people worldwide.

INTRODUCTION

I began my bridge teaching career in Marina del Rey, California in 2001, and moved to Palm Desert, California in 2006. In my new home in the desert, I found a wonderful community of people interested in learning bridge, and others who wanted to update their bridge game with the latest bidding systems.

Many of my students reside in the country clubs and senior retirement communities that dot the Coachella Valley in Southern California. I've taught bridge classes at the Bighorn Golf Club, Indian Ridge, Tamarisk, Mountain View, Trilogy and Andalusia Country Clubs, and at the Segovia Retirement Community and La Quinta Senior Center. I also teach small private groups. My husband and I direct sanctioned duplicate games at the Bighorn Golf Club, Sun City and Trilogy Country Clubs.

In 2007, I decided to write the "*I Love Bridge*" book series as a user-friendly approach to teaching the "nuts and bolts" of the game. I hope the books will be valuable as a teaching tool for bridge teachers, and also function as a workbook for those interested in a self-learning textbook complete with sample hands and quizzes.

I believe students will continue to learn and improve their game if they are comfortable at the beginning of the learning process. This approach works well with my students, and they enjoy the easy-to-read text and practice hands that accompany each lesson.

I've taught the series to many students, and received positive feedback for the class material. After taking Beginning/Refresher classes, many students continue to learn bridge by enrolling in my Intermediate and Advanced classes.

The "*I Love Bridge*" Beginner/Refresher book is designed for beginning bridge players, and for those who have played in the past and want to update their game.

The Intermediate book introduces more complex elements of the game, and reinforces the "Framework of Bidding" point count rules. The book covers notrump responses such as Stayman, Jacoby transfers, Gerber, and quantitative bids. In addition there are chapters on preemptive bidding, balancing seat bids, negative doubles, takeout doubles, declarer play, reverse bidding, and the cross ruff among other topics.

The Advanced book offers many of today's popular conventions such as Lebensohl, Hamilton, control bids and declarer play, and includes the two-over-one game force bidding system.

Bridge is played throughout the world, and offers players exciting competitive events and social gatherings. One of my students was injured and unable to play golf and other sports. Bridge opened a new world of sociability and interest for him. The hugs of thanks from the student and his wife are very special to me, and one of the reasons I love teaching the game of bridge. We learn, have fun, laugh and make new friends – what could be better?

BRIDGE CONDUCT AND ETIQUETTE

An awareness of the following rules is important so that the game is played fairly, making it enjoyable for you and your partner, and the opponents.

- Be courteous toward your partner and the opponents at all times.

- Place value on your bridge partnership, as you are working together as a team. Everyone makes mistakes, and there are decisions to be made in every hand. Respect your partner's decisions even if they turn out to be wrong for one particular bridge hand.

- Try to make all bids or calls in the same tempo, and do not use emphasis in your voice or body language to express approval or disapproval of your partner's or the opponents' bids, calls or plays.

- Do not use facial expressions to show displeasure or happiness at a bid, play or lead by partner. No gloating, high-fives or similar gestures when you get a good result.

- Never try to deceive the opponents by taking more time than necessary in bidding or play of the hand. Try hard not to draw inferences from partner's hesitation in bidding or play.

- Play in a timely fashion, placing cards face up on the table. Do not detach a card from your hand before it's your turn to play. Don't snap the cards or play the cards in a way that obscures players from seeing the card.

- Avoid any conduct or gratuitous comments that could embarrass your partner or the opponents, or interfere with the enjoyment of the game.

- Pay attention during the game.

- Always strive to follow correct American Contract Bridge guidelines in all calls, bids and play of the hand.

CHAPTER ONE

FRAMEWORK OF BIDDING

REFRESHING YOUR POINT COUNT:

High card points (HCP):
Aces = 4 points; Kings = 3 points; Queens = 2 points; Jacks = 1 point.

Length points: Add one point for every card over <u>four cards in a suit.</u>
Example: AK109/<u>52</u> = 7 HCP + 2 length points = 9 points in the suit.

Count both HCP and Length Points to Determine Hand Value.

Modern bidding:
- Open suits on the one-level with a good 12+points.
- Open 1NT with 15-17 points, balanced distribution (Chapter 4).
- Open 2♣ with 22+points (Chapter 5).
- Open 2NT with 20-21 points, balanced distribution (Chapter 5).

Short suit points with a trump fit: In addition to your HCP and length points, add short suit points <u>only after an 8+card fit</u> is found in a suit with partner.

Short suit points

Declarer's short suit points:
      Singletons - 1 card in a suit = 2 points
      Doubletons - 2 cards in a suit = 1 point
      Void - 0 cards in a suit = 3 points

Responder's short suit points:
      Singletons - 1 card in a suit = 2 points
      Doubletons - 2 cards in a suit = 1 point
      Void - 0 cards in a suit = to the number of dummy's trumps.
Example: 3 trumps = 3 points; 4 trumps = 4 points; 5 trumps = 5 points; etc.

Point count for short suit honors in <u>side suits:</u>

With a trump fit, add one point to the **face value** of a singleton honor in a side suit Example: Singleton king = 4 points. However, the ace is the only honor that receives full value of the singleton (2 points), plus the four-point face value of the ace to equal six points. Also, short suit honors in side suits bid by partner may be more valuable.

With no trump fit, discount kings, queens and jacks by a point. Short honors don't fully pull their weight without a trump fit.

Does your opening hand have 2½ quick tricks (QT)?

Quick tricks are aces, kings with queens in the same suit, aces with queens in the same suit, and kings with small cards. Counting quick tricks is another guide to evaluate your opening values. You should open the bidding holding 2½ quick tricks. **Do not** add additional points for quick tricks. The quick trick count is used only as a follow-up check on your opening values. **Queens and jacks standing alone or together are not quick tricks and are called slow tricks.** Holding too many queens and jacks detract from the value of your hand. However, there is more value in a hand with those holdings when kings, aces and tens accompany them.

Example: ♠QJ9, ♥QJ54, ♦<u>K9</u>, ♣QJ83. Although this hand has 12 HCP, the hand may not hold good opening values with only the ♦ **K9 as a ½ quick trick.** Also, the distribution is balanced with the points scattered throughout the suits, offering little ruffing value.

Quick Trick Count

AK = 2 QT
AQ = 1 & ½ QT
A = 1 QT
KQ = 1 QT
Kx = ½ QT

Hand A - Open 1♥	(five-card major)	Hand B - Open 1♣	(no five-card major)
♠9	0	♠AK102	2
♥AQ1085	1 and 1/2	♥K974	1/2
♦KQ109	1	♦54	0
♣987	0	♣Q107	0
	2 1/2 QT		2 1/2 QT

Suggested partnership points needed for games and slams:

Game = 3NT	Three Notrump = 25 - 26 points
Game = 4♠/4♥	Four of a Major = 25 - 26 points
Game = 5♦/5♣	Five of a Minor = 28 - 29 points
Small Slam = 6NT/6♠/6♥/6♦/6♣	Six in a Suit or Notrump = 33 - 36 points
Grand Slam = 7NT/7♠/7♥/7♦/7♣	Seven in a Suit or Notrump = 37 - 40 points

Bonus Points: It's important to recognize that your opening hand facing partner's opening hand should produce game. You only receive bonus points when games or slams are bid.

Part scores: Any contract that isn't a game is defined as a part score.
Many hands do not have the combined partnership points to make games or slams. You can end the auction in a part score when you don't have the required points for game or slam contracts. Part scores receive fewer bonus points than game or slam contracts.

FORCING AND NON-FORCING BIDS: The (+) sign means you may have "more" points in your hand or number of cards in your suit when you bid.

Forcing Bids: When a responder has <u>never passed</u> in the auction, the responder is called a non-passed hand (NPH), and has an <u>unlimited</u> point count. The NPH responder will continue to describe his higher point count on his rebids.

- When a NPH responder has never passed in the auction, and later bids a <u>new suit</u>, responder's bid of the new suit *forces* opener to bid again for one more round of bidding. Each time a <u>new suit</u> is bid by a NPH responder, the bid is *forcing* for opener to bid again for another round of bidding.

- NPH responder's bid of a <u>new suit</u> at the one-level shows four+cards in the suit and 6+points.

- NPH responder's <u>new suit</u> at the two-level shows 10+points and five+cards in the heart suit over a 1♠ bid, or at least 10+points and four+cards in any minor suit.

- A NPH responder does not have to jump at his first opportunity to bid to show a strong hand. Responder first makes *a forcing* bid of a <u>new suit</u> as opener must bid again. If you jump, your bid may take away partner's bidding space. The forcing bid gives opener an opportunity to further describe his hand.

- Opener's <u>only</u> forcing bid is a jump-shift into a new suit, and is forcing to game.

Non-forcing bids: When a player <u>limits</u> his hand, his bids are non-forcing.

- When a responder <u>passes</u> at his first chance to bid in the auction, the player is called a passed hand (PH) responder. All bids by a PH responder are non-forcing as <u>responder has limited his hand to no more than 11 points by his initial pass.</u> Opener may choose to bid or pass.

- When a NPH or PH responder limits his hand by a raise of partner's suit (not a new suit) or bids notrump (not a suit) - <u>these bids are non-forcing.</u> The simple raise (6-10) points, the limit raise (10-12) points, or a 1NT bid (6-10) points, show no less than the lower level in the range, or more than the higher level in the range. These bids are <u>limited</u> bids, as they limit the upper point count of the bid and are called "range" bids.

- A PH responder's bid of a new suit is non-forcing for opener to bid again, as responder has limited his hand by his initial pass. Opener may choose to bid or pass if opener determines the partnership does not have enough points for a game contract or slam contract.

- Opener's bids are generally non-forcing, responder can pass or take a preference to opener's first bid suit, which usually shows a weak hand.

RESPONDER'S OPTIONS *WITH* SUPPORT FOR PARTNER'S OPENING MAJOR.

Option #1: (6-10) points: The simple raise: Three+cards in partner's suit.

Example: Opener 1♠ - Responder 2♠   Raise partner's suit at the two-level.

Option #2: (10-12) points: The limit raise: Three+cards in partner's suit.

Example: Opener 1♠ - Responder 3♠.   Jump to the three-level.

Notice: The 10 point hand is used both for the simple raise and the limit raise.
Explanation: Responder with 10 points and only three-card support, should bid the simple raise at the two-level. Responder with 10 points and four-card support can bid the limit raise, as there is now a known nine-card fit. Responder with 11-12 points and three or four+card support bids the jump limit raise, as the 11-12 point hand is close to an opening hand.

Option #3: 11-15 points: Responder makes a forcing bid of his own suit with **11-12 points**, and later jumps in partner's suit at the three-level with three+card support for partner, inviting partner to bid game in partner's suit. Responder can make a forcing bid of his own suit with an opening hand **of 13-15 points,** then bid game in partner's suit after hearing partner's non-jump rebid.

Option #4: 16+points: Responder makes a forcing bid to learn more about partner's hand, and then may explore for slam.

RESPONDER'S OPTIONS *WITHOUT* SUPPORT FOR PARTNER'S OPENING SUIT.

 Option #5: 6-11 points: A **PH** responder can bid a new suit or notrump at the **one-level** with 6-11 points. Responder needs **10-11 points** to bid a five+card heart suit over 1♠, or any four+card minor at the **two-level**. Responder's jump rebid in his suit shows a six+card suit and **11 points (or a bad 12), invitational.** All these bids are **non-forcing** as responder has originally passed in the auction.

Option #6: 6+points: A **NPH** responder's one-level bid of a new four+card suit is **forcing.** Opener must bid again for one more round of bidding.

Option #7: 10-15points: A **NPH r**esponder must have a five+card heart suit and **10+points** to bid hearts at the **two-level** over a 1♠ bid, and **10+points to** bid any four+card minor suit at the **two-level.** A **NPH r**esponder can bid a new suit at the one-level, and then jump to show a six+card suit and **11-12 points, invitational.** All new suit bids are forcing for one round of bidding. Responder bids 3NT with **13-15 points** and a balanced hand - **non-forcing.**

Option #8: 16+points: Responder makes a forcing bid to learn more about partner's hand, and then may jump-shift to explore for slam.

RESPONDER'S OPTIONS WHEN PARTNER OPENS A MINOR.

Option #9: 6+points: Responder should bid his four+card major after partner's one-level minor opening bid, especially with weaker hands. If responder has four cards in both major suits, responder bids the major suits up-the-line, i.e. the four-card heart suit first, allowing opener to rebid spades on the one-level if opener has a four-card spade suit, keeping the bidding at a low level. **NPH forcing, PH non-forcing.** In some cases with a game forcing hand, responder may bid a minor first, and later bid his four-card major.

Option #10: RESPONDER'S NOTRUMP BIDS: Non-forcing

Responder holds no four+card major, and no support for partner's minor suit opening bid. Responder may have a balanced hand or an unbalanced hand with no other convenient bid.

Responder's bids:	
6-10 points	Bid 1NT
11-12 points	Jump to 2NT - invitational to game
13-15 points	Jump to 3NT - game

 **JUMPS AND JUMP SHIFTS**

REBIDS BY OPENER AND RESPONDER

Opener jumps in his suit to show 16-18 points and a six+card suit...

Example: Opener bids 1♥... Responder bids either 1♠, 1NT or two of a minor...
Opener jumps to 3♥ with 16-18 points holding such as: ♠x ♥AKQxxx, ♦KQx, ♣Qxx.

Responder jumps in his suit at his rebid to show 11-12 points and a six+card suit, <u>Invitational.</u>

Example: Opener bids 1♣... Responder bids 1♥... Then after opener makes a simple rebid, responder jumps to 3♥ with 11-12 points holding such as: ♠xx, ♥AKJxxx, ♦Kxx, ♣xx

---

Opener with support of responder's suit, jumps to game with 19-21 points.

Example: Opener 1♦... Responder bids 1♥...
Opener bids 4♥ holding such as: ♠Axxx, ♥AKQx, ♦KQx, ♣xx (one point - doubleton club).

Partner promised 6+points and four+cards in the suit with his one-level response.
Opener counts 19+6 = 25 points needed for game, and bids 4♥.

In this sequence, hearing a game bid from opener showing 19-21 points, responder may then explore slam possibilities if holding 12+points.

Sample jump hand by opener: 16-18 points
North and South pass throughout the bidding.

West (Dealer)	1♥	1NT		East
♠AK5	<u>3♥</u>	4♥		♠109
♥AK9875				♥Q6
♦Q97				♦J1062
♣9				♣KQ1032

- West opens the bidding 1♥ with 18 points.
- East bids 1NT with 9 points. East does not have three+card heart support for partner's suit, or 10 points to bid 2♣, a new suit at the two-level.
- West JUMPS to 3♥ showing 16-18 points and a six+card heart suit.
- Now East knows there is an eight+card heart fit, and West has shown 16-18 points. East bids the 4♥ game. At least 16 points+9 points = 25 points for game.

Opener jump shifts into a new suit: 19-21 points

- Jump shifts by opener create *game-forcing* auctions.
- The jump shift suit may be a three+card suit in an emergency, but normally shows four cards in the suit.
- Opener can jump rebid to 2NT with <u>18-19 points</u> and a balanced hand. The jump shift into 2NT is NOT a game-forcing auction. Responder can pass with a weak hand.

Sample jump hand by opener: 16-18 points
North and South pass throughout the bidding.

West (Dealer)			East
♠AK652	1♠ 3♥	1 NT 4♥	♠108
♥AKQ2			♥J9864
♦Q92			♦K10
♣7			♣Q1098

- West opens the bidding 1♠ with 19 points.
- East with 7 points (add one point for the fifth heart) bids 1NT. East does not have three-card spade support for partner's suit, or 10+points to bid 2♣, a new suit at the two-level.
- West JUMP SHIFTS to 3♥.
- East has a five-card heart suit, and opener promises at least a four-card heart suit. Now with the heart fit, East adds one point each for the diamond and spade doubletons, or two more points. East bids 4♥ game, knowing the partnership has a nine-card heart fit and 28 points.
- Opener's 19 points+9 points = 28 points.

West's jump shift to 3♥ created a game force and allowed East to reach the 4♥ game.

Responder's jumps: Responder's jumps can show preference bids for partner's suit. Jump rebids in responder's suit shows a six+card suit are natural and invitational.
Responder's jump shift after an initial forcing bid in a new suit shows 17+ points.

Responder first makes a forcing bid of a new suit, and then may jump in partner's suit.

Example: Opener 1♦ - Responder 1♠   Opener 2♣ - Responder 3♦

Responder first makes a forcing bid of a new suit, then may jump shift to show strong two-suited hands:

Example: Opener 1♣ - Responder 1♠   Opener 1NT - Responder 3♥

Responder's immediate jump shift can be preemptive and weak.
Alertable and by partnership agreement. Responder has 0-5 points and a six+card suit.
Example: Opener 1♥ - Responder - 2♠   Weak, opener may pass.

#1 Responder _with_ support for opener.

	Opener	Responder
6-10 points - low	1♠	2♠ Simple raise.
10-12 points - medium	1♠	3♠ Limit raise (usually 4 trumps).
13-15 points - high		Bid a _forcing_ new suit at the one or two-level, and rebid game in partner's suit, after a non-jump rebid by partner.
16+points - highest,		Responder makes a forcing bid to learn more about partner's hand, then may jump shift to explore for slam.

#2 Opener's rebid after hearing support from responder.

	Opener	Responder	Rebids by Opener
12-15 points - low	1♠	2♠	Pass.
16-18 points - medium	1♠	2♠	3♠ Invite game. *
19-20 points - high	1♠	2♠	4♠ Bid game. **

---

* In response to partner's simple raise, **opener can rebid a five+card supported suit** at the three-level with 16-18 points to invite partner to bid game. Responder bids game if he is at the top of his range (8-10 points), or passes if he's at the bottom range (6-7 points).

** Opener jumps to game to show 19-21 points.

Opener can also bid a "help suit" game try (page 15).

#3 Opener's rebid in support of responder's suit.

	Opener	Responder	Rebids by Opener
12-15 points - low	1♥	1♠	2♠ Raise at the two-level.
16-18 points - medium	1♥	1♠	3♠ Bid at the three-level, invite game. *
19-20 points - high	1♥	1♠	4♠ Bid game at the four level. **

---

* Opener jumps at the three-level, invitational, to show 16-18 points and four-card support of responder's suit.

** Opener jumps to game with 19-21 points and four-card support of responder's suit. Responder may explore for slam with slam values after opener's jump to game.

Fourth suit forcing: Conceived by Norman Squire of England, the fourth suit forcing convention was introduced as a waiting bid. When three suits have been bid by the partnership, the fourth suit may be bid as an artificial bid. The fourth suit does not promise a holding in the fourth suit, and is usually played as forcing to game by an NPH responder, and a one round force by a PH responder.

- As responder's jumps are invitational, responder needs the fourth suit forcing bid as a tool to reach game with stronger hands.
- The fourth suit is used when responder has no clear bid.
- Responder may also have a two-suited hand. In standard bidding, the fourth suit could be forcing for one round, however, these days the bid is usually played as forcing to game.
- Fourth suit forcing is helpful in locating the right contract, as opener will be able to clarify his hand type and values economically, knowing he is in a forcing auction.

Sample hand: Fourth suit forcing

West			East
♠ KQ965	1♠	2♣	♠ A4
♥ AQ1043	2♥	3♦ fourth suit	♥ K82
♦ 9	3♥	4♥	♦ 1082
♣ 76			♣ AJ1054

- East can't support the opener's spade suit, or support partner's heart suit with only three hearts, as West could be bidding a 4-card heart suit.
- East's can't jump in his unsupported club suit as that would show six clubs and would not be forcing.
- East uses the 3♦ bid as fourth suit forcing, asking West to clarify his holding in the major suits.
- West's rebid of the heart suit shows 5-5 distribution in the major suits.
- East can now bid the 4♥ game.

Sample hand: Fourth suit forcing

West			East
♠ AQ107	1♣	1♥	♠ KJ8
♥ Q108	1♠	2♦ fourth suit	♥ AKJ43
♦ 952	2♥	4♥	♦ 876
♣ KQ3			♣ 762

- East has enough values for game, however, he can't bid 3NT with three small diamonds, nor jump in his unsupported heart suit, which would show six hearts.
- East uses fourth suit forcing by bidding 2♦, asking West to clarify his holding in the major suits or bid 3NT.
- West can't bid notrump holding three small diamonds, **but can bid 2♥ to show delayed three-card heart support.** East can now bid the 4♥ game.

Help Suit Game Try: Non-alertable

- An opener with 16-18 points may invite partner to bid game in a major after hearing partner's simple raise of the major.
- Opener asks partner if he holds the higher range of his bid, in other words 8-10 points, and a reasonable hand, by bidding a new suit…the help suit… at the three-level.
- Opener has a weakness in the second suit, usually two to three losers, or a three or four-card holding to one top honor is ideal.
- If responder has "help" in the suit, responder will bid game, or lacking help in the suit, responder will merely rebid the major at the three-level.
- Opener's rebid in the major at the three-level can also ask for help in the trump suit.

Examples of help suit side holdings: Jxxx, Qxxx, Kxxx, or Axxx, xxx (xx).
Responder: Responder with 8-10 point determines his help in the suit bid by opener.

- Examples of responder's help in those suits: AK, Ax, KJxx, K10x, Q10xx, x, xx
- Examples of no-help and responder's sign-off in three of the major: xxx, 10xxx, Jxxx
- Holdings of three or four cards to one honor are intermediate holdings…you will be swayed by whether you have a good hand overall. Shortage tends only to be good if you have decent trump length.

Sample hands: Help suit game tries.

#1	West			East
	♠7	1♥	2♥	♠AJ4
	♥AK953	3♦ (help suit)	3♥ (sign-off)	♥752
	♦Q932			♦654 (no help in diamonds)
	♣KQJ			♣A854

#2	West			East
	♠AJ965	1♠	2♠	♠10762
	♥A75	3♥ (help suit)	4♠ (bid game)	♥KQ6
	♦AK3			♦107642
	♣86			♣2

#3	West			East
	♠K87	1♥	2♥	♠A65
	♥A10643	3♣ (help suit)	4♥ (bid game)	♥Q987
	♦AK			♦982
	♣K43			♣QJ7 (help in the club suit)

#4	West			East
	♠KQ10965	1♠	2♠	♠J87
	♥J98	3♥ (help suit)	4♠ (bid game)	♥A106 (A10 useful)
	♦A2			♦K76
	♣A10			♣8754

REVIEW OF THE FRAMEWORK OF BIDDING

 **OPENER**

1. Open suits at the one-level with a good 12 points which includes HCP and length points.

2. The Standard American System requires a five+card major to open a major suit at the one-level.

3. Holding no 5-card major, open a three+card minor.

4. Open 1♦ with four diamonds. Open 1♣ with equal 3-3 in both minors.

5. Don't count short suit points until you find an eight+card fit in a suit with partner.

6. Opener's bids and rebids are usually nonforcing calls.

7. Holding two five-card suits, open the higher-ranking suit first, and bid <u>the suits "down" the line</u>.

8. Don't rebid an <u>unsupported</u> five-card suit as a rebid of the suit shows a six+card suit.

9. You can rebid a five-card <u>supported</u> suit as an invitational bid.

10. Jump shifts in a new suit (19-21 points) create *game-forcing* auctions.

11. Jump shifts to 2NT (18-19 points), are not game forcing.

12. Open 1NT with 15-17 HCP+length points (Chapter 4).

13. Open 2♣ with 22+HCP+length points, or 8 ½ playing tricks (Chapter 5).

14. Open 2NT with 20-21 HCP+length points, balanced hand (Chapter 5).

RESPONDER

1. Responder must keep the bidding open with 6 points which include HCP and length points.

2. A new suit by a NPH responder *is forcing* for opener to bid at least one more time. A PH responder's bids are non-forcing bids.

3. At the one-level, a new suit shows 6+points and four+cards in the suit.

4. At the two-level, a new suit shows 10+points and 5+cards in the heart suit over a 1♠ opener, or four+cards in any minor suit.

5. A NPH responder does not have to jump at his first bid to show a strong hand. Responder makes *a forcing* bid of a new suit, and later shows strength by his rebid.

6. Responding with 4-4 cards in two suits, bid the lower-ranking suit first, and bid the suits "up" the line.

7. When partner opens a minor, responder bids a four+card major before supporting opener's minor. Responder should always bid the four+card major first with a weaker hand.

Exception: With enough points to force to game, responder may bid a five-card minor first, and later introduce the four-card major.

8. Don't count short suit points until you find an eight+card fit in a suit with partner.

9. Don't rebid an <u>unsupported</u> five-card suit, as a rebid of the suit shows a six+card suit. You can rebid a five-card <u>supported</u> suit as an invitational bid.

10. Jump rebids in your suit show six+cards in the suit and 11-12 points, invitational. Jump raises or preference in partner's suit shows three+support and 11-12 points, invitational. Responder can make a forcing bid with 13-15 points, then jump to game in partner's suit after partner's non-jump rebid.

11. Responder with 17+points makes a forcing bid, and with certain strong hands, may jump shift to explore slam possibilities.

12. Responder bids an artificial 2♦ waiting bid in response to opener's 2♣ opening bid (Chapter 5).

The point count rules and concepts in the Framework of Bidding are guides to help your partnership accurately arrive at successful contracts.

As opener you should ask yourself these questions.

- Is my hand a minimum, invitational or strong opening bid?
- What has responder's bid told me about his point count?
- Has responder made a forcing bid?
- Has responder limited his point count by first passing, or bidding a non-forcing support range bid or a notrump bid?

As responder, you should ask yourself these questions.

- Do I need more information from partner? If so, I'll make a forcing bid to learn more about partner's opening hand and point count.
- How high should the partnership bid with the available partnership points?
- What strain of suit or notrump will be the best contract?
- When I re-evaluate my hand with support for partner's suit, are there game values?

CAPTAIN OF THE HAND: Either the opener or responder can become the "captain" of the hand. Being the captain means you are the player who will take charge of the bidding after partner limits his hand.

Example: Opener bids 1♠ Responder bids 2♠ (6-10) points. Responder's 2♠ bid has limited his hand to a maximum of 10 points. Opener as captain, can pass, invite or bid game. However, when opener invites responder to game, responder now becomes the captain as to whether to pass or accept opener's invitation and bid game.

There are sayings in bridge such as "The one who knows goes" (to game), and the one who doesn't know "invites" (partner to game). The Framework of Bidding language creates rules to enable you and your partnership to bid accurately. As you continue to play bridge, you'll understand when you can modify the rules for certain types of hands.

You can bid more aggressively with distributional hands such as 6-5, 5-5, and 5-4 distribution, and with partnership hands holding a known nine+card trump fit. Upgrade your hand with more aces, kings, tens and nines, and with points located in your long suits. This type of hand is a better than a hand holding too many honors in short suits. Your bidding decisions and hand analysis will take into account vulnerability, partner's and the opponents' bids, and the location of your honors in reference to the opponents' bid suits. You may have to lie about your hand at times. Try to select the least "offensive" lie if that's the case.

You'll apply creative thinking in your bidding decisions, and the challenge of applying your analysis of the elements of your hand within the Framework of Bidding process is why bridge remains an exciting and evolving game.

Practice hands: **Answers on page 22.**

#1   North (Dealer)
                                            ♠KQ54
                                            ♥A10
                                            ♦AJ74
                                            ♣642

West   East
♠A86   ♠J2
♥973   ♥J654
♦1086   ♦Q32
♣QJ85   ♣AK107

                                            South
                                            ♠10973
                                            ♥KQ82
                                            ♦K95
                                            ♣93

North is the dealer with _____points and bids____; East passes; South with ____points
bids____; West passes; North bids____; East passes; South bids____; All Pass.
What is the contract____? Who is the declarer____? Who leads the first card____?
What is the lead___?

#2   North
                                            ♠A87
                                            ♥A54
                                            ♦752
                                            ♣6432

West (Dealer)   East
♠K2   ♠QJ9
♥KQ1092   ♥87
♦AQ108   ♦J43
♣108   ♣KQJ75

                                            South
                                            ♠106543
                                            ♥J63
                                            ♦K96
                                            ♣A9

West is the dealer with _____points and bids____; North passes; East with ____points
bids____; South passes; West bids____; North passes; East bids____; South passes; West
bids____; All Pass. What is the contract____? Who is the declarer____? Who leads the first
card____? What is the lead___?

#3

North (Dealer)
♠Q10642
♥AK1062
♦QJ9
♣ ---

West
♠A5
♥Q7
♦K432
♣Q10532

East
♠J7
♥J543
♦65
♣AK974

South
♠K983
♥98
♦A1087
♣J86

North is the dealer with ____points and bids____; East passes; South with ____points
bids_____; West passes; North now with ____points bids____; East passes; South bids____;
All Pass. What is the contract____? Who is the declarer____? Who leads the first card____?
What is the lead___?

#4

North
♠QJ10
♥83
♦Q32
♣KQ842

West
♠9743
♥5
♦KJ1076
♣J103

East
♠A52
♥K62
♦A985
♣765

South (Dealer)
♠K86
♥AQJ10974
♦4
♣A9

South is the dealer with _____points and bids ____; West passes; North with ____points
bids____; East passes; South bids____; West passes; North bids_____; All Pass.
What is the contract____? Who is the declarer____? Who leads the first card____?
What is the lead___?

#5

North (Dealer)
♠108
♥J642
♦J108
♣Q853

West
♠964
♥K975
♦Q542
♣J7

East
♠AKQJ32
♥A103
♦ ---
♣K1064

South
♠75
♥Q8
♦AK9763
♣A92

North is the dealer and passes; East with ___points bids____; South with ____points bids____;
West with ____points bids____; North passes; East bids_____: All Pass.
What is the contract____? Who is the declarer____? Who leads the first card____?
What is the lead___?

#6

North
♠Q62
♥Q6
♦K103
♣AQ983

West
♠A1073
♥742
♦J85
♣1062

East
♠854
♥KJ9
♦A742
♣J54

South (Dealer)
♠KJ9
♥A10853
♦Q96
♣K7

South is the dealer with _____points and bids ____; West passes; North with ____points bids____; East passes; South bids_____: West passes; North bids_____; All Pass.
What is the contract____? Who is the declarer____? Who leads the first card____?
What is the lead___?

Answers to practice hands on pages 19 - 21.

#1

North is the dealer with 14 points and bids 1♦; East passes; South with 8 points bids 1♥; West passes: North bids 1♠; East passes; South bids 2♠; All Pass.

North is declarer in 2♠. East leads the ♣A.

#2

West is the dealer with 15 points and bids 1♥; North passes; East with 11 points bids 2♣; South passes; West bids 2♦; North passes; East bids 2NT; South passes; West bids 3NT; All Pass.

East is declarer in 3NT. South leads the ♠4.

#3

North is the dealer with 14 points and bids 1♠; East passes; South with 9 points (1 point for the doubleton heart) bids 2♠; West passes; North now with 17 points (3 points for the club void) bids 3♦ help suit game try, invitational. East passes; South with 9 points and help in the diamond suit accepts the game invitation and bids 4♠. All Pass.

North is declarer in 4♠. East leads the ♣A.

#4

South is the dealer with 17 points and bids 1♥; West passes; North with 11 points bids 2♣; East passes; South jumps to 3♥; West passes; North bids 4♥; All Pass.

South is declarer in 4♥. West leads the ♦J.

#5

North is the dealer and passes; East with 19 points bids 1♠; South with 15 points overcalls 2♦;West with 6 points bids 2♠; North passes; East now with 22 points (three points for diamond void) bids 4♠; All Pass.

East is declarer in 4♠. South leads the ♦A.

#6

South is the dealer with 14 points and bids 1♥; West passes; North with 14 points bids 2♣; East passes; South bids 2NT; West passes; North bids 3NT; All Pass.

South is the declarer in 3NT. West leads the ♠3.

CHAPTER TWO

THE FINESSE

The finesse is a form of declarer play of taking tricks by capturing an opponent's honor between declarer's lower and higher honors.

- The finesse allows you to make extra tricks by capturing opponent's honors. When you finesse, you play one defender for a certain card holding

- A good way to know if you should finesse is to ask yourself how it would help you if your opponent covers your honor with their honor.

- **The finesse gives you a 50% chance of capturing an opponent's honors.**

Examples: #1.Dummy   #2. Dummy   #3. Dummy
         QJ6-lead Q   **J**83- lead J   105**3** - lead 3

          Declarer   Declarer   Declarer
          A108**7**   AQ10**9**   **K**82

- #1   Play the queen from dummy. If RHO covers your queen or jack with his king, **covering an honor with an honor,** you will play the ace of the suit and capture RHO's king. **The finesse is successful.**

- #2   Play the jack from dummy. RHO may **not** have the king, in which case he will not cover the jack, and you will allow the jack to **"RIDE"** into your LHO's hand by playing a low card from your hand and **not** playing the ace. If LHO has the king, you have lost the finesse. Always finesse from the hand where you will want to repeat the finesse if it wins.

Play a low card up to your honor:

- #3   You are playing RHO for the ace in the suit. Play a low card from dummy **toward the king, the card you want to win the trick**. If RHO plays the ace, your king will be a good trick. If RHO plays low, you will insert your king.

- If you lead the king of your suit, there is a 100% chance an opponent will capture your king with his ace. However, if you lead a low card **toward your king**, playing your RHO for the king, and RHO plays the ace, your king will be a good trick. If he does not play his ace, your king wins.

You need three tricks in the suit:

Example: North
                            ♠AQ<u>10</u>
              West   East
              ♠KJ96   ♠832
                            Declarer
                            ♠75<u>4</u>

- In the above example, you need three tricks in the suit.
- Play declarer's ♠4 to the ♠10 in dummy. If the ♠10 wins the trick, return to your hand, and next lead low to the ♠Q in the suit.
- Lead up to the lower-ranking card first; leading to cards you hope will win tricks.

Do not finesse by leading out an unsupported queen unless you also have the jack in the suit. Even then there may be alternative plays.

Example: Dummy   Declarer
         <u>A</u>8762   Q54<u>3</u>

Lead the three from your hand toward the ace in dummy. Then play the six in dummy towards the queen in your hand, playing your RHO for the king, and with Q543 facing AJ76 lead to the jack rather than leading out the queen.

Finesse by leading towards double honors with a holding such as KQ2 facing 963:

> **Why?** If declarer leads a low spade **towards** the ♠KQ in dummy, LHO may play the ♠A, and dummy's ♠KQ will be good tricks. If LHO does **not** play the ♠A, declarer returns to his hand to lead again toward dummy's ♠KQ.

Defense to the finesse:

- A commonly used phrase in bridge is to **"Cover an honor with an honor"**.
- **Only cover an honor with an honor if it will possibly promote a trick your hand or partner's hand, for example, the jack or 10 of the suit.** Do not cover an honor when the J109 are exposed in the dummy, as there is no card to promote for the defense. **Usually cover the second of touching two touching honors played from dummy.**

Examples: Dummy leads the ♠Q
#1 Dummy   Defender
    ♠QJ108   ♠K32
                                  Do not cover - nothing to promote, dummy holds 10.
#2 Dummy leads the ♠Q   Defender
    ♠QJ95   ♠K63
                                  Do not cover the queen. Cover the jack with king when next led - may promote partner's 10.

Finesse Combinations

Dummy	Declarer	
AK2	J106	Lead the jack, if it wins there are no losers in the suit.
A73	**Q**J10	Lead the queen, and if it wins, repeat the finesse by leading the jack.
KJ10	87**2**	Lead low and play the 10 in dummy if LHO plays low. If the 10 loses to the ace, return to your hand and lead low to the jack, playing LHO for the queen.
AQ95	J106	Lead the jack and if the jack wins, repeat the finesse by leading the 10.
AJ10	98**6**	Lead low and play the 10 if LHO plays low. If the 10 loses to the king or queen, return to your hand and play low to the jack, finessing against the other honor.
K96	J108	Lead the jack and play low if LHO plays low; if the jack loses to the ace, return to your hand and repeat the finesse.
Q94	**A**32	Play the ace, then play low towards the queen. DON'T lead the queen!
AQ10	84**2**	Lead low toward the 10, then return to your hand and finesse the queen, hoping your RHO does not have both the jack and the king.
AQJ109	**8**	Ruffing finesse: Lead the 8 to the ace and then lead the queen, hoping North has the king. If RHO covers your queen with the king, you ruff and if not, you discard a loser from your hand.
KQJ107	---	Ruffing finesse: Lead the king from dummy, hoping RHO has the ace, and if it is covered, ruff. If RHO doesn't cover, discard a loser from your hand.
A65	Q**10**9	Lead the 10, play low from dummy when LHO plays low. If the 10 loses to the jack, lead the queen to finesse LHO for the king.
KQ65	74**3**	Lead the three from your hand, playing your LHO for the ace. If your king wins the trick, return to your hand to play a low card toward the queen. If the finesse loses to the ace you can try to set up the 13th card in the suit for an extra trick later.
AJ53	**K**876	With an 8-card fit, the queen will not usually fall. Finesse LHO for the queen, playing the king first, and then finessing the jack. 'Eight ever, nine never".
A754	**J**1098	Double finesse two missing honors. Lead the jack and if LHO plays low, play low from dummy. If RHO plays an honor, next play the 10 and finesse LHO for the other honor.

Sample finesse hand:

Contract: 4♠   West leads the ♣10

Bidding: East and West pass throughout the bidding.

South (Dealer)	North
1♦	1♥
1♠	4♠

North
♠QJ54
♥AQ103
♦AQ8
♣J3

West
♠6
♥KJ8
♦K53
♣**10**98742

East
♠K1082
♥972
♦1076
♣Q65

South (Dealer)
♠A973
♥654
♦J942
♣AK

- South opens the bidding 1♦ with 12 points. North with 16 points bids 1♥, bidding the major suits up the line. South bids 1♠. North now knows there is at least an eight-card spade fit. North adds South's minimum 12 opening points to his 16 points showing at least 28 game points. North bids 4♠.

- **South counts four possible losers. Two hearts, one diamond, and one spade. South must finesse for the ♠K, ♥K-J and the ♦K.**

- After winning the ♣10 in his hand with the ♣A, South leads the ♦J. West covers the ♦J with the ♦K. The finesse of the ♦K is successful, however West covering the ♦J with the ♦K promotes East's ♦10.

- South draws defenders' trumps. Dummy plays the ♠Q, East the ♠2, South the ♠3 and West the ♠2. Declarer continues the ♠J from dummy; East covers ♠J with the ♠K, covering the second honor played from dummy. Declarer play the ♠A. The spade finesse is successful, however East has promoted the ♠10 in his hand by covering the ♠J. South **does not** draw East's last trumps, instead plays a low heart to the ♥10 in dummy, which wins the trick. South plays a low spade from dummy towards his ♠9 finessing against East's ♠108. Declarer now plays a low heart to the ♥Q in dummy.

South loses one spade and one diamond making an overtrick in the 4♠ contract.

THE FINESSE:

The finesse is a form of declarer play of taking tricks by capturing an opponent's honor between declarer's lower and higher honors.

The simple finesse gives you a 50% chance of capturing an opponent's honors. In general, lead <u>toward</u> the card you hope to take the trick.

A good way to know if you should finesse is to ask yourself how it would help you if your opponent covers your honor with their honor.

Finesse by leading towards double honors. Play a low card up to your honors with e.g. 962 facing either K74 or KQ4.

- If you lead the king of your suit, there is a 100% chance an opponent will capture your king with his ace.

- Lead a low card **toward your king in your hand**, playing your RHO for the ace. If RHO plays the ace, your king will be a good trick.

Do not finesse by leading out an unsupported queen unless you also have the jack in the suit.

Example: Dummy   Declarer
       A76   Q54**3**

- Lead the three from your hand toward the ace in dummy, then play the six in dummy towards the queen in your hand, playing your RHO for the king.

Defense to the finesse:

- Only cover an honor with an honor if it will promote a trick in either your or your partner's hand, for example the jack or 10 of the suit.

- Usually cover the second of two honors played from dummy.

#1   North
                                      ♠62
                                      ♥J92
                                      ♦K8
                                      ♣AKJ432

West   East (Dealer)
♠AKJ543   ♠1097
♥108   ♥AQ
♦32   ♦AQJ964
♣Q109   ♣75

                                      South
                                      ♠Q8
                                      ♥K76543
                                      ♦1075
                                      ♣86

East is the dealer with _____points and bids____; South passes; West bids____; North bids____; East bids ____; South passes; West bids____; North passes; East bids____; All Pass. What is the contract____? Who is the declarer____? Who leads the first card____? What is the lead____?

#2   North
                                      ♠K765
                                      ♥Q65
                                      ♦QJ106
                                      ♣76

West (Dealer)   East
♠AQJ   ♠1084
♥K984   ♥AJ72
♦A73   ♦942
♣AJ10   ♣KQ9

                                      South
                                      ♠932
                                      ♥103
                                      ♦K85
                                      ♣85432

West is the dealer with ____points and bids____; North passes; East with ____points bids____; South passes; West bids____; All Pass. What is the contract____? Who is the declarer____? Who leads the first card____? What is the lead____?

#3

North
♠AK9
♥10863
♦J106
♣AQJ

West (Dealer)
♠J64
♥K74
♦K854
♣K107

East
♠8752
♥J
♦A972
♣8643

South
♠Q103
♥AQ962
♦Q3
♣952

West is the dealer and passes; North with _____points bids_____; East passes;
South bids_____ (transfer); West passes; North bids_____; East passes; South bids_____;
West passes; North bids_____; All Pass. What is the contract_____? Who is the declarer_____?
Who leads the first card_____? What is the lead_____?

#4

North
♠Q94
♥A6
♦J9
♣KQ9742

West (Dealer)
♠A6
♥KQJ1042
♦Q85
♣J10

East
♠KJ87
♥9853
♦A1032
♣3

South (Dealer)
♠10532
♥7
♦K764
♣A865

West is the dealer with _____points and bids_____; North with _____points overcalls_____;
East bids_____; South passes; West bids_____; All Pass.
What is the contract_____? Who is the declarer_____? Who leads the first card_____?
What is the lead_____?

Answers from finesse hands pages 27 - 29.

#1

East is the dealer with 15 points and bids 1♦; South passes; West bids 1♠;
North overcalls 2♣; East rebids 2♦; South passes; West jumps to 3♠; North passes;
East bids 4♠; All Pass.
West is the dealer in 4♠. North leads the ♣A.

West's possible losers are two clubs, one heart, one diamond, and a possible spade loser if
trumps do not break. After winning the ♣A and ♣K, North plays a third club hoping partner
can over-ruff the dummy. South duly over-ruffs with the ♠Q.
South leads the ♠8 -- with no better choice available. West wins in his hand and leads a
low diamond to the ♦Q in dummy. The finesse wins and a possible losing heart is sluffed
on the good diamonds in dummy.

#2

West is the dealer with 19 points and bids 1♣; North passes; East with 10 points bids 1♥;
South passes; West bids 4♥; All Pass.
East is the declarer in 4♥. South leads the ♣8.

With the 8-card heart fit, you will finesse your RHO for the ♥Q. 'Eight ever, nine never".
Play the ♥K first in dummy, and next play a low heart toward the ♥AJ72 in your hand.

#3

West is the dealer and passes; North with 15 points bids 1NT; East passes; South bids 2♦
(Jacoby transfer to hearts); West passes; North bids 2♥; East passes; South bids 3NT; West
passes; North bids 4♥; All Pass.
North is declarer in 4♥. East leads the ♠8.

North plans to finesse the ♥K by playing a low heart to his ♥Q in the dummy. North will
also finesse West for the ♣K. One finesse wins and one loses. North makes his contract,
losing a heart and two diamonds.

#4

West is the dealer with 15 points and bids 1♥; North with 14 points overcalls 2♣; East with 10
points jumps to 3♥; South passes; West now with 16 points bids 4♥; All Pass.
West is declarer in 4♥. North leads the ♣K. West has one heart loser, one club loser and
can't afford two diamond losers. West must play South for the ♦K by playing a low diamond to
his ♦Q, successfully finessing against South's ♦K

BRIDGE CONCEPTS   **DRURY**   **LEADS IN SUIT CONTRACTS**

 BRIDGE CONCEPTS:

Quality hands: Quality hands have good intermediates or "spot" cards in long suits such as the 1098 in: AK<u>1098</u> is a better suit than AK<u>542</u>.

Honors in long suits have more value: The honors help small cards become tricks. Example:

Good   ♠AK986   ♥KQ76   ♦932   ♣2   HCP in longer suits, 5-4 distribution.

Fair   ♠Q87   ♥QJ6   ♦AK2   ♣J982   HCP in short suits, balanced, with no ruffing value.

Declarer should take a moment to plan the play of the hand after the opening lead, and before playing to the first trick.

Count losers in suit contracts: In a suit contract, declarer counts how many **losing tricks** there are in the declarer and dummy hands, and decides on a plan to discard losers on a long side suit, or trump losers when void in those suits.

Count winners in notrump contracts: In notrump contracts, declarer counts the number of **winning tricks** in the declarer and dummy hands to determine the number of additional tricks needed to make the contract. Winning tricks are aces, aces and kings in the same suit, and running suits such as the AKQJ.

 Responder's magical fourth trump card creates the nine+card fit.

After partner's one-level major suit opening, responder may choose not to make a jump limit raise with **10 points** holding only three trumps.

- The simple raise of an opening bid should be (6-10) points. Responder with 10 points, a balanced hand and **only three trumps** should bid the hand as a simple raise, or bid a new suit, and then raise to three of partner's major if he has another bid. However, responder with three trumps and 11-12 points may give the three-level jump limit raise.

- With 10-12 points and **four trumps**, responder knows there is at least a nine-card fit, which allows a jump limit raise at the three-level according to the **"law of total tricks"**. **The law of total tricks indicates you can usually bid to the level of the combined trump fit.** The extra fourth trump in dummy strengthens declarer's ability to make the three-level contract with a minimum hand, and also allows the partnership to compete to the three-level in a competitive auction.

Weak freaks:

Preemptive jump at the four-level holding five+trump support.

- Partner has opened a major showing five+cards in the suit. Responder with no more than 6-10 points and five+cards in partner's major, can bid a preemptive jump to game in the major. This bid is called a **weak freak.**

- **By using the law of total tricks, the partnership can bid the four-level game with a combined 10+cards in the trump suit. The four-level jump does not show an opening hand**. Opener passes unless holding enough points to investigate slam. The four-level preemptive raise is designed to prevent opponents from finding their contract. Use the higher point count range when vulnerable.

HAND VALUE RULES of 20 and 15:

The rule of 20:

Hands with long suits have more trick-taking potential than balanced hands. The Rule of 20 can help you determine if a two-suited hand with fewer than 12 HCP is good enough to open.

- Count your HCP and the length of your two longest suits. Open the hand if the total count equals at least **20.** Points should be in your two longest suits.
  Example: ♠AJ10764 ♥KQ97 ♦109 ♣2
  You have ten HCP plus ten cards in your two longest suits = 20. Open 1♠.

The rule of 15: The Rule of 15 is used only <u>in fourth seat</u> after three passes.

- You are in fourth seat after three passes. Count your HCP and the number of cards in your **spade suit**. Open the hand if the <u>**number of spades plus your HCP equals 15.**</u>
  Example: ♠KJ1076 ♥KQ9 ♦J96 ♣2
  You have 10 HCP + five-cards in your spade suit. 10+5 = <u>15</u>. Open 1♠.

OPENING POSITIONS:

First, second and fourth* seat opening bids should have full opening values. However, you may open the bidding in third seat after two passes with a good five+card suit and 8+points.

> **Why:** In third seat, your partner and your RHO have passed. There may be an even distribution of points in all four hands, and both partnerships can make a part score, or your LHO may have a big hand.

You want to open "light" in third seat with 8+points and a good suit to help partner get off to a good lead, or to find a part score. Drury is a convention to determine if partner has opened light in third seat (see page 33).

(*Fourth seat may be opened light similar to a third seat opening with partnership agreement).

THE DIFFERENT FACES OF DRURY
All forms of Drury must be alerted.

Drury is a conventional response by a passed hand after partner opens a major in third seat after two passes. Partner may open "light" in third seat with less than an opening bid and a good five+card suit. Drury may also be used when partner opens light in fourth seat after three passes with partnership agreement. The lesson deals only with third seat light openings.

- Opening light in third seat is valuable since the player in fourth seat may have a good hand, and your light opening may act as a preemptive bid.

- You can give partner lead information if opponents win the contract.

- Drury enables responder to show a limit raise with 10-12 points and three+card support in opener's major. The use of Drury keeps the bidding low at the two-level.

- There is no need to jump at the three-level to show the limit raise, as a jump to the three-level may get you too high in the contract when third seat opener is light.

- Drury is used only after major suit openings.

- Drury bids are conventional and must be **alerted.**

Opener bids 1♥/1♠ in third seat after two passes.
Responder bids 2♣ - a Drury bid to show a limit raise of partner's suit.

Standard or reverse Drury can be used in conjunction with two-way Drury with partnership agreement.

Standard Drury:
Standard Drury's rebid by opener of 2♦ shows a light opener, and 2♠ or 2♥ shows an opening hand.

Reverse Drury:
Reverse Drury is by far the most popular current variation of standard Drury, where a rebid of 2♦ shows a full opener, and 2♠/2♥ shows a light hand.

Two-Way Drury:
Two-way Drury uses a **2♦** bid by responder to show a four-card limit raise, and a **2♣** bid to show a three-card limit raise.

Drury is played in competition:
When 1♥ or 1♠ is doubled, or 1♥ is overcalled by 1♠, responder may use Drury when available, by partnership agreement.

Responder bids a 2♣ <u>reverse</u> Drury bid after opener bids 1♥/1♠ in third seat after two passes.

Opener's responses to reverse Drury:

Bid 2♠/2♥ - third seat minimum opening.
Bid 2♦ - full opener with five+spades or hearts.
Bid 4♠/4♥ - bid game with 16 - 18 points.
Bid 2♥ - after 1♠ opener, 2♥- shows a minimum with five spades
      and four or more hearts.

Bid 2NT - full opener and a balanced hand.
Bid 3♠/3♥ - jump of opener's major, an invitational slam try.
Bid 3NT- natural – stronger and giving a choice of 4♠, (4♥) or 3NT game

---

Sample reverse Drury hand: Contract 2♠   East leads ♥3
Bidding:

South (Dealer)	West	North	East
Pass	Pass	1♠	Pass
2♣ (reverse Drury)	Pass	2♠	All Pass

North
♠KQ1076
♥Q109
♦Q9
♣J87

West
♠94
♥AJ62
♦J43
♣K1054

East
♠532
♥K74**3**
♦A85
♣A32

South (Dealer)
♠AJ8
♥85
♦K10762
♣Q96

- South and West pass
- North bids 1♠. East passes.
- South bids 2♣ - **<u>Reverse Drury</u>** - asking if North has an opening bid, showing a limit raise and 3+card spade support.
- North bids 2♠ showing a light third seat opener.
- South passes.
- Declarer will lose two hearts, a diamond and two clubs making the 2♠ contract.

#1

North (Dealer)
♠9
♥AQ73
♦A982
♣10876

West
♠K6532
♥84
♦73
♣QJ53

East
♠Q1074
♥52
♦Q654
♣AK9

South
♠AJ8
♥KJ1096
♦KJ10
♣42

North is the dealer and passes; East passes; South bids____; West passes;
North bids_____ reverse Drury; East passes; South bids____; West passes; North bids____;
All Pass. What is the contract____? Who is the declarer____? Who leads the first card____?
What is the lead___?

#2

North
♠K107
♥85
♦Q82
♣AJ876

West (Dealer)
♠Q942
♥A632
♦J4
♣K105

East
♠53
♥KQJ74
♦A1053
♣32

South
♠AJ86
♥109
♦K976
♣Q94

West is the dealer and passes; North passes; East bids____; South passes;
West bids___ reverse Drury; North passes; East bids____; All Pass.
What is the contract____? Who is the declarer____? Who leads the first card____?
What is the lead___?

#3

North (Dealer)
♠K1097
♥K952
♦109
♣A96

West
♠---
♥Q1076
♦KJ543
♣Q732

East
♠QJ32
♥J43
♦AQ8
♣J54

South
♠A8654
♥A8
♦762
♣K108

North is the dealer and passes; East passes; South bids_____; West passes;
North bids_____ reverse Drury; East passes; South bids_____; All Pass.
What is the contract_____? Who is the declarer_____? Who leads the first card_____?
What is the lead___?

#4

North
♠KQ1076
♥AJ10
♦AQ9
♣84

West
♠54
♥Q962
♦J4
♣K7532

East
♠93
♥K743
♦8532
♣AJ9

South (Dealer)
♠AJ82
♥85
♦K1076
♣Q106

South is the dealer and passes; West passes; North bids_____; East passes;
South bids_____ reverse Drury; West passes; North bids___; All Pass.
What is the contract_____? Who is the declarer_____? Who leads the first card_____?
What is the lead___?

Answers to Reverse Drury practice hands on pages 35 - 36.

#1

North is the dealer and passes; East passes; South bids 1♥; West passes;
North bids 2♣ (reverse Drury); East passes; South bids 2♦; West passes; North bids 4♥;
All Pass. The contract is 4♥. South is the declarer. West leads the ♣Q.

- South's 2♦ reverse Drury response shows a **full** opening hand.
- Declarer must finesse East for the ♦Q to make his contract.

#2

West is the dealer and passes; North passes; East bids 1♥; South passes;
West bids 2♣ (reverse Drury); North passes; East bids 2♥; All Pass.
The contract is 2♥. East is the declarer. South leads the ♦6 low from an honor.

- East's 2♥ bid shows **less** than an opening bid.

#3

North is the dealer and passes; East passes; South bids 1♠; West passes;
North bids 2♣ (reverse Drury); East passes; South bids 2♠; All Pass.
The contract is 2♠. South is the declarer. West leads the ♦3.

#4

South is the dealer and passes; West passes; North with 17 points bids 1♠; East passes;
South bids 2♣ (reverse Drury); West passes; North bids 4♠; All Pass.
The contract is 4♠; North is the declarer. East leads the ♥3.

- North reevaluates his hand to 18 points and bids 4♠ after hearing South's
  Drury limit raise in spades.

NOTES

When you are defending, you get to fire the first shot by your opening lead. Choosing the opening lead is one of the harder parts of the game. Listed below are possibilities you can consider when leading to the first trick.

OPENING LEADS IN SUIT CONTRACTS:

Lead top of a sequence: A sequence is two or more cards in a <u>contiguous sequence</u>. When you lead top of a sequence you hope to take winners for your side before declarer can somehow get rid of his losers. Or **you** want to **"knock out"** an opponent's higher card in the suit, and promote your honor in the suit.
Example: <u>A</u>Kxxx   <u>K</u>Qxx   <u>J</u>1076   <u>Q</u>J43

Lead from an interior sequence: Defined as a sequence with a non-touching honor.
Example: Lead the jack from K<u>J</u>1098, or a broken interior sequence K<u>J</u>986.

Leads in partner's suit: Lead the ace, or low from an honor. Lead top of nothing from any three+card holding with no honors in the suit if you have raised the suit, otherwise lead low.

It is fine to lead the top card of a doubleton if partner has bid the suit.
Example of top of a doubleton: <u>9</u>8   <u>5</u>3   <u>8</u>6

Why? When you lead a doubleton in partner's suit, you can **"signal"** partner you have only two cards in the suit by playing a <u>**high card first and then a low card**</u> the next time the suit **is played.** You hope you will subsequently be able to trump the third round of the suit. When partner has **not bid the suit,** be a wary of making the doubleton lead -- especially from an honor, as the lead may help the opponents set up their long suit.

When you have supported partner's suit, or he has raised your suit, lead the king from A<u>K</u> in partner's suit. The lead of the king shows the ace or a king-queen in the suit. Lead low from three or four cards to an honor in partner's suit, or with no honor in the suit, lead your highest card. **Since you have supported the suit, the lead will usually not be a confused with an initial doubleton.**

Example: K7<u>2,</u> <u>8</u>764

Lead singletons: Lead singletons other than in the trump suit.

Why? The singleton lead may be in an opponent's side suit or partner's suit. You hope to trump an opponent's high cards, or partner's low cards in that side suit, once you become void in the suit. Leading a singleton in the opponent's trump suit, however, may cause partner to lose a high trump card, as declarer is last to play to the trick, and may have a higher honor and capture partner's honor card.

Lead low from an honor: Leading a low card tends to show you may have an honor in the suit. You can signal your partner you may have a <u>high card in a suit by leading a low card in the suit.</u> For example, leading low from a king may be a good lead, as only the ace is higher and your partner may have the queen to force out opponent's ace.

Lead "top of nothing": Spot cards are the 10 down to the 2. Leading a high "spot" card usually denies an honor in the suit. **You can signal you have <u>nothing in a suit by leading a high card in the suit.</u>** A lead of a top of nothing card does not necessarily show a doubleton. However, don't lead the 10 from e.g. 1063; lead low.

Example: top of nothing leads - <u>8</u>65, <u>7</u>632

Usually don't lead a<u>way</u> from an ace in a suit contract.

If you must lead the suit, lead the ace or don't lead the suit. Try not to lead away from **unsupported aces** unless partner has bid the suit.

Example: Unsupported aces - Axxx. Supported aces - AKxx - the king supports the ace.

Why? If you lead low from an ace, declarer may have a singleton in the suit, and will trump your ace when the suit is next played. Aces are generally used to capture kings.

Don't lead away from an AQ in a suit contract.

If your original holding, which included AQ or AJ is located over declarer, your honors may be poised to capture declarer's king, allowing your secondary honor also to win a trick -- so long as you haven't led the suit and set up declarer's king for a trick. AQ are generally used to capture kings.

Opponents' suits:

- Lead dummy's first bid suit if you must lead a suit bid by the opponents. Leading through strength is better than leading through weakness in dummy.
- Lead trump when you have a holding in a long side suit bid by declarer, as declarer may try to use dummy's trumps to ruff out the suit. This is especially so when declarer ends up in his second suit, and when you don't have an obvious lead in a side suit. Leading a trump also applies when declarer has shown three suits.
- Lead a trump when opponents make a sacrifice bid. A sacrifice bid usually relies on trumping suits to make extra tricks.
- A trump lead may be a good lead when the opponent's final contract ends in opener's second suit. The bidding has shown there may be few cards in declarer's first suit in the dummy. For example, when responder has taken a preference for opener's second suit after his initial response in a new suit or 1NT. As responder did not have at least three+cards to support opener's first bid suit, he is probably showing two or fewer cards in the first suit, so leading a trump may prevent declarer ruffing his first bid suit.

Leads to avoid in suit contracts:

- The opponents' suits unless indicated by the bidding.
- An unsupported ace or from an AQ in a suit not bid by partner, or an ace in a suit that may be a void suit.
- Leading away from honors in a grand slam or notrump slam contract.
- Avoid leading doubletons unless you have trump control in the opponent's suit, and may get a later ruff from partner.

What do you lead in a suit contract?

1. ♠QJ108_____

2. ♦KJ108_____

3. ♥Q852_____

4. ♠AK642_____

5. ♠98 (partner's suit)_____

6. ♥KQJ65_____

7. ♠J1096_____

8. ♠AJ109_____

9. ♥8765_____

10. ♦K82_____

11. ♥K32_____

12. ♠AK43_____(partner's suit)

13. ♥9876_____

14. ♣A864_____

15. ♦KQ108_____

16. ♠AQ85_____

17. ♠J8_____(partner's suit)

18. ♣8_____

19. ♠AK_____

20. ♣K875_____

21. ♥Q876_____

22. ♠KJ972_____

 Answers:

1. ♥**Q**J108   top of a sequence
2. ♦K**J**108   interior sequence
3. ♥Q85**2**   low from Qxxxx
4. ♠**A**K642   ace from AK
5. ♠**9**8   partner's suit.
6. ♥**K**QJ65   top of a sequence.
7. ♣**J**1096   top of a sequence
8. ♠AJ109   ace if bid by partner, or don't lead.
9. ♠ **8**765   top of nothing.
10. ♦K8**2**   low from an honor.
11 ♥K3**2**   partner's suit

12. ♠A**K**43   lead the king first if bid by partner.
13. ♥**9**876   top of nothing.
14. ♣**A**864   no other lead or suit bid by partner.
15. ♦**K**Q108   top of a sequence.
16. ♠AQ85   don't lead the suit unless bid by partner.
17. ♠**J**8   partner's suit, high-low.
18. ♣**8**   any singleton except trump.
19. ♠A**K**   king from AK doubleton
20. ♣K87**5**   low from an honor.
21. ♥Q87**6**   low from an honor.
22. ♠K**J**972   top of interior broken sequence.

CHAPTER THREE
THE BOTTOM LINE

 ### BRIDGE CONCEPTS:

Quality hands: Quality hands have good intermediates or spot cards.
Honors in long suits have more value: The honors help small cards become tricks.

Count losers in suit contracts.
Count winners in notrump contracts.

Responder's magical fourth trump card creates the nine+card fit:
A responder's jump limit raise should be analyzed as to whether responder holds three or four trumps and 10 or 11-12 points for the limit raise.

The rule of 20: Modern bidding emphasizes long suits and two-suited distributional hands. The rule of 20 is a point count system to help evaluate some opening hands. Count your HCP and the length of your two longest suits. **Open the hand if the count equals <u>20.</u>**

The rule of 15: The rule of 15 is used with only the spade suit in borderline hands in **<u>fourth-seat</u>** after three passes. Count your HCP and the number of cards in your spade suit.
Open 1♠ if the number of your spades and HCP equal 15.

Opening positions: First, second and fourth seats should have full opening value hands. However, you may open the bidding in third seat after two passes with a good five+card suit and 8+points less than a traditional opener.

Weak freaks: A preemptive four level jump holding five+card trump support and no more than 6-10 HCP after partner opens one of a major.

OPENING LEADS IN SUIT CONTRACTS:

Lead top of a sequence or interior sequences.

Leads in partner's suit: Lead the ace or low from an honor, or lead top of nothing from any three+card holding with no honors in the suit you have raised, otherwise lead low.

Lead the top card of doubletons if partner has bid the suit. Your high-low play of the cards has "<u>signaled</u>" partner you have a doubleton in the suit. You will be able to trump the suit when the suit is led a third time.

Lead singletons: Singletons are good leads except usually in the opponent's trump suit.

Leads in side suits: Leading a <u>low card</u> led indicates you may **<u>have an honor</u>** in the suit.

Lead top of nothing: Spot cards are non-honor cards such as the 9, 8, 7, etc.
When you lead a **<u>high "spot" card</u>** you tend to deny an honor in the suit.

#1

North

♠983

♥Q842

♦AJ8

♣Q75

West

♠QJ1042

♥103

♦952

♣AK9

East

♠A76

♥J7

♦Q743

♣J1042

South (Dealer)

♠K5

♥AK965

♦K106

♣863

South is the dealer with _____points and bids; West overcalls_____; North bids_____; East bids_____; South passes; West passes; North bids_____; All Pass.
What is the contract_____? Who is the declarer_____? Who leads the first card?
What is the lead___?

#2

North (Dealer)

♠AQ876

♥KJ732

♦76

♣3

West

♠K9

♥54

♦KQ54

♣A8765

East

♠43

♥A109

♦J1032

♣K1042

South

♠J1052

♥Q86

♦A98

♣QJ9

North is the dealer with _____points and bids_____; East passes; South with _____points bids_____; West passes; North now with _____points bids_____; All Pass.
What is the contract_____? Who is the declarer_____? Who leads the first card?
What is the lead___?

#3

North
♠A72
♥Q532
♦107
♣K852

West
♠Q65
♥A987
♦K64
♣Q103

East
♠KJ1098
♥10
♦AQ983
♣64

South (Dealer)
♠43
♥KJ64
♦J52
♣AJ97

South is the dealer and passes; West passes; North passes; East with _____points and using the rule of 15 bids____; South passes; West bids____; All Pass.
What is the contract_____? Who is the declarer_____? Who leads the first card?
What is the lead___?

#4

North
♠75
♥KJ1098
♦AQ7
♣852

West
♠J9
♥54
♦K543
♣QJ764

East
♠AKQ32
♥632
♦J8
♣A103

South (Dealer)
♠10864
♥AQ7
♦10962
♣K9

South is the dealer and passes; West passes; North in third seat with _____points bids_____;
East with _____points bids_____; South bids _____; All Pass.
What is the contract_____? Who is the declarer_____? Who leads the first card?
What is the lead___?

#5

West
♠AK102
♥J97
♦2
♣AK1096

North
♠53
♥K2
♦AK1043
♣8743

East
♠J984
♥Q843
♦875
♣Q2

South (Dealer)
♠Q76
♥A1065
♦QJ96
♣J5

South is the dealer and passes; West with _____points bids_____; North with _____points overcalls_____; East passes; South bids _____; All Pass.
What is the contract_____? Who is the declarer_____? Who leads the first card?
What is the lead____?

#6

North
♠1052
♥KJ987
♦876
♣A8

West
♠K984
♥53
♦K943
♣Q96

East (Dealer)
♠AQJ76
♥6
♦J52
♣K1032

South
♠3
♥AQ1042
♦AQ10
♣J754

East is the dealer and uses the rule of 20 and bids_____; South with _____points overcalls_____;
West with _____points bids_____; North bids_____; All Pass.
What is the contract_____? Who is the declarer_____? Who leads the first card?
What is the lead____?

Answers to practice hands on pages 44 - 45.

#1

South is the dealer with 14 points and bids 1♥; West overcalls 1♠; North bids 2♥; East bids 2♠; South passes; West passes; North bids 3♥ (North knows there is a nine-card fit and competes to the three-level; All Pass.

South is the declarer in 3♥. West leads the ♠Q.

2

North the dealer with 10 HCP points and two 5-card suits uses the rule of 20 and bids 1♠; East passes; South with 10 points jumps to 3♠; West passes; North now with 15 points bids 4♠; All Pass.

North is the declarer in 4♠. East leads the ♦J.

#3

South is the dealer and passes; West passes; North passes; East with 10 points and five spades uses the rule of 15 bids 1♠; South passes; West bids 2♠; All Pass.

East is the declarer in 2♠. South leads the ♥4.

#4

South is the dealer and passes; West passes; North in third seat with 11 points bids 1♥; East with 15 points bids 1♠; South bids 2♥; All Pass

North is the declarer in 2♥. East leads the ♠A.

#5

South is the dealer and passes; West with 16 points bids 1♣; North with 11 points overcalls 1♦; East passes; South bids 3♦; All Pass.

North is the declarer at 3♦. East leads the ♣Q.

#6

East is the dealer, using the rule of 20, and bids 1♠; South with 16 points (two points for the singleton spade) overcalls 2♥; West with 9 points bids 2♠; North bids 4♥ (weak freak); All Pass.

South is the declarer in 4♥. West leads the ♠4.

CHAPTER FOUR   NOTRUMP BIDDING

STAYMAN   JACOBY TRANSFERS   QUANTITATIVE BIDS

NOTRUMP LEADS

OPEN 1NT WITH 15-17 High Card Points
No singletons - No voids - Only one doubleton
No short suit points

Your distribution is balanced, holding only one possible doubleton. You can add value to your hand by counting length points, however, you must have 15 -17 high card points before adding any length points.

Count Winners in Notrump Contracts:

Before playing to the first trick in a notrump contract, declarer should count the **winning tricks** in the declarer and dummy hands to determine the number of additional tricks needed to make the contract. Winning tricks are running suits such as AKQJ, ace, or ace and king in the same suit in both the declarer and dummy hands.

Example: Declarer: ♠AKJ10 ♥J85   ♦A83 ♣A54 = 4 winners - ♠AK ♦A ♣A

Dummy: ♠987   ♥A432   ♦KJ2 ♣KJ10 = 3 winners - ♥A   ♦K ♣K

- There are seven winners in the above example in the declarer and dummy hands. Declarer knows two more tricks are needed to make nine tricks and the 3NT contract.

After partner opens 1NT, responder with 10-14 points should immediately recognize the hand will be a game-level contract.

The Stayman Convention:

A 2♣ artificial bid by responder shows he has at least one four-card major, and asks the 1NT opener to bid his four-card major if he has one.

Responder must have 8+points to bid Stayman:

Why use Stayman? It is generally best to have the strong hand become the declarer and be the concealed hand. Also, it's usually best for declarer to play last to the first trick, and have the lead come into the strength in declarer's hand.
- After a 1NT opening, the partnership does not rule out playing in a 4-4 major fit.
- **Opener does not have to announce or alert the Stayman bid to the opponents.**

Opener with a four-card major: Opener bids the four-card major, or holding both majors, bids the majors "up the line".

Responder:

- **8-9 points:** <u>With</u> opener's major, three-level bid to <u>**invite**</u> a major game.
- **10-14 points:** <u>With</u> opener's major, bid a major game.
- **8-9 points:** *Without* opener's major, bid 2NT to <u>**invite**</u> a 3NT game.
- **10-14 points:** *Without* opener's major, bid a 3NT game.

Opener *without* a four-card major: Opener with no four-card major bids 2♦. The 2♦ <u>artificial</u> bid denies a major and the partnership will typically play in a notrump contract.

After opener's 2♦ response:
Responder:

- **8-9 points:** Bid 2NT to <u>**invite**</u> game in 3NT.
- **10-14 points:** Bid game in 3NT.

Exception to responder's use of Stayman with a balanced hand.

Responder may <u>**not**</u> want to use Stayman with 4-3-3-3 or 3-4-3-3 balanced hand. Raise to 2NT with 9 points or bid 3NT with 10-14 points. Although you have a four-card major, your hand is balanced with no ruffing value. The hand will probably play better in a notrump contract.

<u>Jacoby Transfers:</u> Jacoby transfers are used to show a <u>five+card major.</u>

Why use Jacoby transfers: Just as in Stayman, it is generally best to have the strong hand be the declarer and the concealed hand. Also, it's usually best for declarer to play last to the first trick, and have the lead come into the strength in declarer's hand. Responder can use Jacoby transfers with a weak hand with less than 8 points. Jacoby transfers are different than Stayman, which requires at least 8+points.

Responder's Jacoby transfers bids:

- Responder bids 2♦, the suit <u>directly</u> below the heart suit, to show the five+card heart suit.
- Responder bids 2♥, the suit <u>directly</u> below the spade suit to show the five+card spade suit.

The 1NT opener must <u>**announce the transfer immediately**</u> upon hearing responder's artificial bid of the transfer suit, and before opener's RHO passes. The <u>partner</u> of the player making the artificial bid <u>always</u> announces or alerts partner's artificial bids. <u>**The player making the conventional bid never announces or alerts his own bid.**</u>

1NT opener's bids after hearing the transfer suit:

- Opening 1NT bidder **MUST** accept the transfer. Opener knows responder has a five+card major, but he might possess a game or slam hand of 10+points, an invitational hand, or a weak hand with 8 or fewer points.

Responder's rebids after opener accepts the Jacoby transfer:

0-8 points and five+card suit:
- Responder passes with a weak hand after the transfer, and opener plays the contract in the transferred suit. Responder's weak hand will usually play better as dummy in the transferred major than in a 1NT contract.

9 points and five+card suit:
- Responder can bid 2NT after the transfer. The 2NT bid invites opener to play in the transferred suit at the three or four-level, pass his 2NT bid, or bid 3NT.

10-14 points and five+card suit:
- Responder can **jump to 3NT** after the transfer bid with a game going hand. The jump to 3NT gives opener the option to play in 3NT or correct to the major game with three+card support in the transferred suit.

8-9 points and six+card suit:
- Responder rebids a six+card suit inviting game in the suit.

10-14 points and six+card suit:
- Responder jumps to game in the transferred suit.

Opener's rebids:

15-16 points:
- Opener passes responder's invitational 2NT bid with two cards in the transferred major, or corrects to three of the major holding three+cards in the major. With a 16-count opener has discretion to go low or high.

16-17 points:
- Holding only two cards in the transferred major, opener bids 3NT after responder's invitational 2NT bid.

16-17 points:
- Opener with three-card support for the transferred major can correct to game in the major after a 2NT invitational bid, or 3NT jump bid by responder.

Although holding three-card support in the major, opener may also decide to play in a 2NT or 3NT contract with a balanced hand with no ruffing value, and no weak side-suit. A source of tricks in a side-suit may also help persuade him to play in notrump.

Super-Accept: 16-17 points+ four-cards in the transferred suit.

- Opener must have a <u>good 16 or 17 points and four-cards in the transferred suit to super-accept the transfer.</u>

- Opener super-accepts by jumping at the three-level of the transferred major suit. After the super-accept by opener, responder can reevaluate his hand, count short suit points, bid game or pass with a weak hand.

Example:

(Dealer)

West		2♥ (transfer to spades)	East
♠AKQ4	1NT		♠108753
♥J107	3♠ (super accept)	4♠	♥A9
♦AK9			♦J754
♣954			♣K2

After the super-accept by West, East can upgrade his nine points to eleven points by adding two points for the doubletons in the club and hearts suits. East bids 4♠.

After partner opens 1NT, responder with 10-14 points should immediately recognize the hand will be a game-level contract. The partnership can explore a major fit with the use of Stayman or Jacoby transfers, however, when no major fit is found, the partnership will tend to play in a 3NT contract.

Quantitative Bids:

4NT response to a 1NT opener: Slam invitational bid by responder.

- Partner opens 1NT in a 15-17 point count range.

- Responder with good 15 points or a bad 16 balanced hand, jumps to 4NT to invite the opening 1NT bidder to bid 6NT with 17 points, the top of his notrump range.

- Responder with 17 points can jump directly to 6NT. **Responder knows the partnership has 32 points (17+15= 32), and bids the 6NT slam.**

- The Gerber ace/king asking convention may be used to determine the number of aces and kings held by opener (Chapter 5).

Rules used by declarer in notrump contracts:

Rule of 11: Counting cards in a notrump contract.

- Declarer's LHO may be leading the fourth card down from his longest and strongest suit in a NT contract.
- If that is the case, declarer subtracts the number of the card led from the number **11**.
- **The answer is the number of cards <u>higher</u> in the dummy, declarer's RHO, and in declarer's hand.**

Example:

North
♠A92

West   East
♠K108<u>7</u>   ♠653

South (Declarer)
♠QJ4

The ♠7 is led. Subtract the ♠7 from the number 11 to give you the number 4.

- Using the rule of 11, South knows there are four cards higher than the ♠7 in the dummy, in the East hand, and in the South or declarer's hand.
- Since dummy and declarer have four cards higher than the ♠7, this leaves East with no cards higher than the ♠7. Dummy's ♠9 will win the trick

Rule of 7:

Declarer is in a 3NT contract, and has only the ace as a "stopper" in a suit.
When to duck or not play the ace in a NT contract. Subtract the number of cards in the suit in the declarer and dummy hands from the number <u>7</u>**.

Example: If there are five-cards in the suit in the declarer's and the dummy's hand.

Use the Rule of 7: Deduct the number of cards in the sample hand on page 44 from the number seven which gives you the number **2**. Declarer should not play the ace for **two rounds of suit, or duck the ace twice unless he fears a shift through another suit even more.**

- By ducking, declarer hopes to deplete RHO in the suit. If RHO later gains the lead, RHO won't able to return his partner's suit to possibly defeat the contract.

**First use the rule of 11: Declarer can determine if his LHO is leading is from a four or five-card suit. If the lead is from a four-card suit, declarer may decide <u>not</u> to use the rule of 7, as ducking the ace will not deplete RHO of the suit.

Sample hand using the rules of 7 and 11:

West leads ♦4 - Fourth card down in West's long diamond suit.
Contract: 3NT
Bidding:

South (Dealer)	West	North	East
1NT	Pass	2♣ (Stayman)	Pass
2♦ (no 4-card major)	Pass	3NT	All Pass

```
                        North
                        ♠AQ104
                        ♥A743
West                    ♦105              East
♠J95                    ♣652              ♠873
♥Q102                                     ♥J96
♦QJ843                                    ♦K96
♣109                                      ♣A843

                        South (Declarer)
                        ♠K62
                        ♥K85
                        ♦A72
                        ♣KQJ7
```

<u>Rule of 11</u>: **Subtract ♦4 from the number 11 to give you the number 7.**

- South counts the rule of **11 minus the ♦4 (lead) = 7.** There are seven cards higher than the ♦4 in the dummy, the East hand and in the South or declarer's hand.
- Declarer counts four diamonds higher than the ♦4 in the dummy and in his hand. This leaves East with **three cards higher than the ♦4.**

South has only the ♦A as a diamond stopper.

<u>Rule of 7</u>: **Subtract the total number of diamonds in both the dummy and declarer hands from the number 7, which gives you the number 2 in the above sample hand.**

- South counts a total of five diamonds in the declarer and dummy hands.
- The number **7 minus five-cards = 2.**
- **Declarer will duck the ♦A for two rounds of the diamond suit, winning the third round of the suit.**
- By using the rule of 7 and 11, South has depleted East of the diamond suit.
- When East wins the ♣A, East has no more diamonds to lead to West.
- Had declarer taken the first or second diamond, East's lead of a diamond to West allows West to run the diamonds and defeat the contract.

<u>OPENING LEADS IN NOTRUMP CONTRACTS:</u>

As a defender in a notrump contract, you want to make an opening lead to set up tricks in your longest suit before declarer is able to set up declarer's long suit. The notrump declarer will possibly have a long minor suit to run to make his contract, or he may simply need to knock out high cards from his side's long suit(s).

- You **may** lead away from an ace in a notrump contract.

  Why? As there is no trump suit, it is safe to **under-lead the ace of a suit, as no one will be able to ruff away your ace**.

- Lead **the 4th card down in your longest and strongest suit.**
  Example: K108<u>7</u>4.

- Lead top of a **three-card sequence** to promote lower honors in the suit.
  Example: KQJ32. This principle extends to leading from a two-card sequence if you have builders below (such as KQ1092).

- Holding only a **two-card sequence**, lead the 4th card down in your long strong suit.
  Example: KQ7<u>6</u>5.

- Lead the top interior card of a sequence. K**J**109,
  or top card from and interior broker sequence K**J**987,

Leads to avoid in notrump contracts:

- Short suits unless bid by partner.

- Suits bid by declarer.

- Honors in short suits.

Exceptions to fourth highest (4th card down) leads:

- When partner has bid a suit, and you have no entries in your hand to your long suit, then lead partner's suit.

- Opponents have bid your long suit.

- Your long suit has three touching honors such as **K**QJxx, **Q**J10xx, **J**1098x. Lead the top of the three-card sequence. Equally, from **K**Q10, **Q**J9 or **J**108, lead the top card from a broken sequence.

What do you lead in a notrump contract?

1. ♠J1096_____

2. ♥A1076_____

3. ♠J643_____

4. ♠Q532_____

5. ♥K8765_____

6. ♠KQJ10_____

7. ♦KJ98_____

8. ♣J109_____

9. ♠K10653_____

10. ♦AQ108_____

11. ♠A9765_____

12. ♦QJ1087_____

13. ♠J10762_____

14. ♦10986_____

15. ♠AKQ10_____

16. ♣QJ76_____

 Answers:

1. ♠**J**1096   top of a three-card sequence
2. ♥A107**6** 4th from longest and strongest
3. ♠J64**3**   4th from longest and strongest
4. ♠Q53**2**   4th from longest and strongest
5. ♥K87**6**5 4th from longest and strongest
6. ♠**K**QJ10 top of a three-card sequent
7. ♦K**J**98   top of an interior broken sequence
8. ♣**J**109   top of a broken sequence

9. ♠K106**5**3 4th from longest and strongest
10. ♦AQ10**8** 4th from longest and strongest
11. ♠A97**6**5 4th from longest and strongest
12. ♦**Q**J1087 top of a three-card sequence
13. ♠J107**6**2 4th from longest and strongest
14. ♦**10**986   top of a three-card sequence
15. ♠**A**KQ10   top of a three-card sequence
16. ♣QJ7**6**   4th from longest and strongest

Open 1NT with 15-17 HCP
No Singletons - No Voids - Only One Doubleton - No Short Suit Points

 **AT A GLANCE**

NOTRUMP BIDDING WITH NO 4-CARD MAJOR SUITS:

Opener bids	Distribution	Points
1NT	Balanced hand. No voids. No singletons. Only one doubleton.	15-17 points
Responder bids 2NT	No four or five-card major, or balanced hand with 4-3-3-3 or 3-4-3-3 distribution. Invite game.	9 points
3NT	Bid game.	10-14 points
4NT	Invite slam.	15-16 points
6NT	Bid slam.	17-18 points

NOTRUMP BIDDING WITH FOUR OR FIVE+CARD MAJOR SUITS:

OPENER	BIDS	POINTS
Balanced distribution. Stayman response with no four-card major. Stayman response, bid major, or with both majors, bid majors "up the line". Jacoby transfer response.	1NT 2♦ response to Stayman. 2♥ first with both majors. Must accept the transfer.	15-17 points
RESPONDER No four-card major No major, invite game. No major, bid game	**BIDS** Pass 2NT 3NT	**POINTS** 0-8 points 9 points 10-14 points
With four-card major. Bid three of the major. Bid four of the major.	2♣ Stayman. 3/♥♠ 4/♥♠	8+points 9 points 10-14 points
Jacoby transfer, with five+card major, bid suit below major	2♦ transfer to ♥ 2♥ transfer to ♠	0+ points

#1   North
                                          ♠KQJ4
                                          ♥AJ10
                                          ♦6532
                                          ♣107

West   East
♠105   ♠8762
♥Q93   ♥875
♦J87   ♦K109
♣KQJ98   ♣643

                                          South (Dealer)
                                          ♠A93
                                          ♥K642
                                          ♦AQ4
                                          ♣A52

South is the dealer with ____points and bids____; West passes; North with ____points
bids____; East passes; South bids____; West passes; North bids____; All Pass.
What is the contract____? Who is the declarer____? Who leads the first card____?
What is the lead____?

#2   North
                                          ♠AK8
                                          ♥Q764
                                          ♦1093
                                          ♣KJ4

West   East
♠109   ♠6543
♥532   ♥J9
♦A852   ♦K76
♣Q1076   ♣9832

                                          South (Dealer)
                                          ♠QJ72
                                          ♥AK108
                                          ♦QJ4
                                          ♣A5

South is the dealer with _____points and bids ____; West passes; North with ____points bids
____; All Pass. What is the contract____? Who is the declarer____? Who leads the first
card____? What is the lead____?

#3

North
♠Q643
♥Q64
♦K1093
♣K4

West
♠K107
♥1082
♦QJ64
♣Q72

East
♠AJ52
♥J97
♦7
♣J9853

South (Dealer)
♠98
♥AK53
♦A852
♣A106

South is the dealer with _____points and bids____; West passes; North with ____points bids____; East passes; South bids____; West passes; North bids____; All Pass. What is the contract____? Who is the declarer____? Who leads the first card____? What is the lead____?

#4

North
♠82
♥AK109
♦A1064
♣J106

West
♠KJ765
♥J653
♦32
♣73

East
♠Q43
♥Q7
♦K75
♣98542

South (Dealer)
♠A109
♥842
♦QJ98
♣AKQ

South is the dealer with ____points and bids ____; West passes; North with ____points bids____; East passes; South bids____; West passes; North bids____; All Pass. What is the contract____? Who is the declarer____? Who leads the first card____? What is the lead____?

#5

North
♠62
♥KQ83
♦Q32
♣A1086

West (Dealer)
♠AKQ4
♥J107
♦AK9
♣954

East
♠108753
♥A9
♦J754
♣K2

South
♠J9
♥6542
♦1086
♣QJ73

West is the dealer with _____points and bids_____; North passes; East with _____points bids_____; South passes; West bids_____; North passes; East bids_____; All Pass.
What is the contract_____? Who is the declarer_____? Who leads the first card_____?
What is the lead_____?

#6

North
♠Q64
♥AJ432
♦72
♣Q109

West
♠95
♥Q5
♦QJ1093
♣J864

East
♠AJ87
♥1098
♦K854
♣75

South (Dealer)
♠K1032
♥K76
♦A6
♣AK32

South is the dealer with _____points and bids_____; West passes; North with _____points bids_____; East passes; South bids_____; West passes; North bids_____: East passes; South bids_____; All Pass.
What is the contract_____? Who is the declarer_____? Who leads the first card_____?
What is the lead_____?

#7

North
♠QJ6
♥842
♦AKQ
♣A1063

West
♠1074
♥J653
♦1064
♣954

East
♠532
♥K107
♦J972
♣Q82

South (Dealer)
♠AK98
♥AQ9
♦853
♣KJ7

South is the dealer with _____points and bids ____; West passes; North with _____points bids___; East passes; South bids____; All Pass.
What is the contract____? Who is the declarer____? Who leads the first card____?
What is the lead____?

#8

North
♠J874
♥A93
♦Q97
♣A102

West (Dealer)
♠A1063
♥KQ2
♦A106
♣K85

East
♠K9
♥J10764
♦543
♣Q96

South
♠Q52
♥85
♦KJ82
♣J743

West is the dealer with ____points and bids____; North passes; East with ____points bids____; South passes; West bids____; All Pass. What is the contract____? Who is the declarer____? Who leads the first card____? What is the lead____?

Answers to practice hands on pages 56 - 59.

#1

South is the dealer with 17 points and bids 1NT; West passes; North with 10 points
Bids 2♣ (Stayman); East passes; South bids 2♥; West passes; North bids 3NT; All Pass.
South is declarer in 3NT. West leads the ♣K.

- Duck the lead of the ♣K twice, and after winning the ♣A, lead a heart to
  dummy's ♥10.
- Declarer has nine tricks if he can establish a third heart trick safely, so forgoes
  the diamond finesse into the "danger" hand.

#2

South is the dealer with 17 points and bids 1NT; West passes; North with 13 points
and holding a balanced hand bids 3NT; All Pass.

South is the declarer in 3NT. West leads the ♣6.

#3

South is the dealer with 15 points and bids 1NT; West passes; North with 10 points
bids 2♣; East passes; South bids 2♥; West passes; North bids 3NT; All Pass.
South is the declarer in 3NT. West leads ♦4.

#4

South is the dealer with 16 points and bids 1NT; West passes; North with 12 points
 bids 2♣; East passes; South bids 2♦; West passes; North bids 3NT; All Pass.
South is the declarer in 3NT. West leads the ♠6.

**South uses the rule of #7 to duck the spade suit twice, depleting East of the
spade suit. Then he takes the diamond finesse into the safe hand.**

#5

West is the dealer with 17 points and bids 1NT; North passes; East with 9 points bids 2♥ (Jacoby transfer); South passes; West bids 3♠ (super-accept); North passes; East bids 4♠; All Pass.

West is the declarer in 4♠. North leads the ♥K.

- East can re-evaluate his hand hearing the super-accept from West adding one point each for the doubleton heart and club suits, now holding a total of eleven points. Had West not made a super-accept, East would have passed 2♠.

#6

South is the dealer with 17 points and bids 1NT; West passes; North with 10 points bids 2♦ (Jacoby transfer); East passes; South bids 2♥; West passes; North bids 3NT; East passes; South bids 4♥; All Pass.

South is the declarer in 4♥. West leads the ♦Q.

#7

South is the dealer with 17 points and bids 1NT; West passes; North with 16 points bids 4NT (quantitative); East passes; South bids 6NT with 17 points and the top of his 1NT bid; All Pass. South is the declarer in 6NT. West leads the ♥3.

- South wins the ♥Q, and tests the diamonds, which do not break. South plays dummy ♣A, then the ♣10 to finesse East for the ♣Q. The finesse is successful
- South makes the 6NT contract with three spades, two hearts, three diamonds and four clubs.

#8

West is the dealer with 16 points and bids 1NT; North passes; East with 7 points bids 2♦ (Jacoby transfer); South passes; West bids 2♥; All Pass.

North leads the ♠4.

NOTES

CHAPTER FIVE

SLAM BIDDING   CONTROLS   BLACKWOOD   GERBER

🏵Open 2♣: 22 + Points or 8 1/2 Playing Tricks

22+HCP and Length Points: The 2♣ bid is an artificial bid and shows 22+points and is *forcing* for one round of bidding.

8 1/2 Playing Tricks: Example: ♠AKQJ1065, ♥AQ9, ♦83, ♣4

◆ 2♦ Response to 2♣ Opening Bid: Bids 2♦, an artificial <u>waiting</u> bid*.

- **Responder must bid even with zero points.** Responder's 2♦ bid is an artificial bid which keeps the bidding open allowing opener to rebid his suit or bid 2NT.
- Responder can rebid 3♣ at his second turn over 2♥ or 2♠ to show a weak hand With 0-3 points (3♦ serves the same purpose over a 3♣ rebid by opener).
- Responder can introduce or rebid his own suit or respond to opener's suit by raising the suit. When opener rebids 2NT, responder may bid Stayman, Jacoby transfers or make a notrump raise. *There are many partnership agreements for responding to 2♣ opening bids. This lesson deals only with the above popular version.

Blackwood Convention: 4NT Bid Asks for Aces and Kings.

Blackwood is used as a tool to find out the number of aces and kings held by the partnership. If you are missing two aces you may bid to a hopeless slam. Either opener or responder may initiate Blackwood. **Certain bidding sequences don't allow for suit agreement, and in those cases, the last suit bid naturally is considered to be the agreed trump suit.**

4NT bid asks for aces	5NT bid asks for kings
Responses	Responses
5♣ - 0 aces or 4 aces	6♣ - 0 kings or 4 kings
5♦ - 1 ace	6♦ - 1 king
5♥ - 2 aces	6♥ - 2 kings
5♠ - 3 aces	6♠ - 3 kings

In addition to the ace and king count, you also need to protect against unguarded side suits. After suit agreement, hands with losers in side suits may require **"control"** bids in those suits before launching into Blackwood.

Controls are bid after suit agreement, or with no suit agreement, the last suit bid naturally is considered the trump suit.

 **Italian Style Control Bids:**

Italian Style control bids are used to show **first and second round suit controls**, and are an invention of the Italian Blue Team. Control bids in the past had shown only first round controls, however, **showing both first and second round suit controls is a superior way of bidding these slam tries.**

Controls have been described as cue bids, however, **control bids** is the ACBL official term for these bids, and is to be used only in suit contracts.

First and second round suit controls:

- First round controls: Aces and voids

- Second round controls: Singletons and kings

Level of controls bids:

- First and second round controls usually begin at the four-level, however may begin at the three-level.

- When bidding controls, bid your cheapest control first.

- Five-level bids usually show only first round controls.

Controls are bid after suit agreement in a game-forcing auction. For slam tries, it's important to know that partner has a control when holding two or more losing cards in a suit. **If there is no suit agreement, the last bid suit naturally is considered to be the trump suit agreement.**

Example:

West (Dealer)	East
1♠	2♦
3♠	4♣ control in clubs
4♦ control in diamonds	4NT Blackwood
5♥ two aces	6♠

In the above hand, East can't agree on the spade suit by bidding 4♠, as it would show only game values and would close the auction. Spades is the last suit bid naturally by West; therefore East's bid of 4♣ shows spade agreement and a control in the club suit - looking for slam. The 4♣ bid cannot be Gerber, as Gerber is usually a jump to 4♣ after a 1NT or 2NT opening bid.

Bidding sequence:

- Control bids are bid <u>up the line, or the cheapest suit first</u>.
- When a player bypasses a suit, he denies a control in the suit.

Example:

West (Dealer)	East
2♣	2♦
2♥	3♥ - slam interest
4♣	4♥
	All Pass

- The heart suit is established.
- West bypasses the spade suit by bidding first or second round control of the club suit.
- East has no spade control and signs off in 4♥.
- Using control bids is a good way to avoid slam holding two fast losers in a suit.

Sample control bid hand: North and South pass in the bidding.
Bidding:

West (Dealer)	East
2♣	2♦ (waiting bid)
2♠	3♠ (slam interest)
4♦ (diamond control)	4♠ (no club control, sign off in game)

West (Dealer)	East
♠AK1098	♠QJ762
♥AKJ	♥Q103
♦AK6	♦QJ8
♣32	♣106

- West opens the bidding with 2♣ showing 22+points.
- East responds 2♦ - a waiting bid. West bids 2♠.
- East bids 3♠ establishing the spade suit as trump, and showing slam interest.
  (East would bid 4♠ to end the auction with only game values).
- **The stronger your hand, the <u>slower</u> you go.**
- West bids 4♦ showing diamond control. East signs off in 4♠.
- West by-passed the club control, so East knows there may be two club losers.
- East passes. Using control bids is a good way to avoid slams holding unguarded side suits in both declarer and responder's hands.

Sample hand: East and West pass throughout the bidding.

Contract: 6♠   West lead ♣7

Bidding:

South (Dealer)	North
2♣	2♦ (waiting)
2♠	3♠ (slam interest)
4♣ (club control)	4♦ (diamond control)
4NT (Blackwood)	5♣ (zero aces)
6♠	All Pass

```
                        North
                        ♠J972
                        ♥QJ64
                        ♦KQ8
                        ♣108

West                                              East
♠4                                                ♠653
♥95                                               ♥8732
♦A10653                                           ♦J9
♣76532                                            ♣QJ94

                        South   (Declarer)
                        ♠AKQ108
                        ♥AK10
                        ♦742
                        ♣AK
```

South is the dealer with 22 points bids 2♣. North with 9 points bids 2♦ (waiting).

- South bids 2♠. North now with 10 points (one point for the doubleton club) bids 3♠, **slam invitational.** North could have closed the auction at 4♠ with only game values. The stronger your hand, the **slower** you go.
- South bids 4♣ - control of the club suit. North bids 4♦ - control of the diamond suit.
- South with the heart suit under control, bids 4NT Blackwood.
- North bids 5♣ (no aces). South only missing one ace, bids 6♠; All Pass.
- Declarer counts his losers in a suit contract. There may be one or two diamond losers.
- After winning the club lead declarer draws trumps ending in his hand.

Lead toward or up to honors in a suit.

- South now leads toward the ♦KQ in dummy, finessing West for the ♦A. If West plays the ♦A, dummy's ♦KQ, will be winning tricks. If West plays a low diamond (not taking his ♦A), South will play the ♦K in dummy. South returns to his hand with the ♣K and leads a diamond toward the ♦Q in the dummy to make his slam, limiting the defenders to one diamond trick.

2NT Opening Bid: 20-21 points.

- Open <u>2NT</u> with <u>20-21 points</u> and a balanced hand, with no voids, no singletons, and at most, one doubleton. A 2NT bid by opener is not forcing. Responder can pass with a balanced hand and 0-4 points.
- Responder can bid Stayman at the three-level to ask partner to bid his four-card major.

> - 3♣ Stayman bid asks for a four-card major
> - Jacoby transfers shows a five+card major
> - 5-11 points: Bid 3NT with a balanced hand.
> - 12+points: Explore for slam

Gerber Convention over Opening 1NT and 2NT: Bid 4♣ Ace/ King asking bid.

- After opening 1NT and 2NT bids, responder's **jump to 4♣ is Gerber** and asks opener for the number of aces and kings in his hand. Holding all four aces, 5♣ is Gerber asking for kings. The Gerber convention is used instead of Blackwood over a 1NT or 2NT opening bids, as a jump to 4NT is quantitative (Chapter 3) inviting partner to bid 6NT. Gerber can be used in conjunction with Stayman and Jacoby transfers.
- **Gerber should not be used with a void, and is <u>always a jump to 4♣</u>.**

Gerber - Bid 4♣ - Ace ask Aces	5♣ King ask Kings
Response	Response
4♦ - 0 or 4 aces	5♦ - 0 or 4 kings
4♥ - 1 ace	5♥ - 1 king
4♠ - 2 aces	5♠ - 2 kings
4NT - 3 aces	5NT - 3 kings

North (Dealer)				South	
♠AK109	1NT		2♣	♠QJ87	
♥AJ9	2♠		4♣ (Gerber)	♥K10	
♦K108	4♠		6♠	♦AQJ52	
♣Q102				♣K7	

North opens 1NT and bids 2♠ in response to South's 2♣ Stayman bid. Gerber is used instead of Blackwood asking for aces, as a 4NT bid would be considered a Quantitative bid denying a spade fit. **As in Blackwood, the last suit bid naturally is considered to be the trump suit.** North bids 4♠, two aces. South bids 6♠.

Gerber must be a <u>jump</u> to 4♣ or it is not Gerber:

Example: 4♣ bid that is not Gerber:

West	East
2NT	3♣ (May be Stayman)
3♦	4♣

East did not jump to 4♣, so the bid should be considered a club suit and not Gerber.

OPENER BIDS 2♣: 22 + points or 8 1/2 playing tricks:

RESPONDER 2♦: A waiting bid to 2♣ opening bid:

OPENER OPENS 2NT: 20-21 points - balanced hand

Responses to 2NT opener:

3♣ Stayman bid asks for a four-card major.

Jacoby transfers shows a five+card major.

5-11 points: Bid 3NT with a balanced hand.

12+ points: Explore for slam.

Blackwood Convention:
4NT bid asks for Aces/Kings.

4NT bid asks for aces	5NT bid asks for kings
Responses	Responses
5♣ - 0 aces or 4 aces	6♣ - 0 kings or 4 kings
5♦ - 1 ace	6♦ - 1 king
5♥ - 2 aces	6♥ - 2 kings
5♠ - 3 aces	6♠ - 3 kings

Gerber Convention over opening 1NT and 2NT:
4♣ Bid Asks for Aces/Kings.

4♣ bid asks for aces	5♣ bid asks for kings
Responses	Responses
4♦ - 0 or 4 aces	5♦ - 0 or 4 kings
4♥ - 1 ace	5♥ - 1 king
4♠ - 2 aces	5♠ - 2 kings
4NT - 3 aces	5NT - 3 kings

Control Bids:

- First round controls: Aces and voids.
- Second round controls: Singletons and kings.

#1   North (Dealer)

                      ♠AQJ

                      ♥AQ6

                      ♦A109

                      ♣KQ109

West   East

♠652   ♠1094

♥9874   ♥K2

♦J54   ♦8763

♣732   ♣J864

                    South

                    ♠K873

                    ♥J1053

                    ♦KQ2

                    ♣A5

North is the dealer with _____ points and bids_____; East passes; South with _____points bids _____ (waiting) bid); West passes; North bids_____; East passes; South bids_____(Stayman); West passes: North bids_____; East passes; South bids_____; West passes; North bids_____; East passes; South bids_____; West passes; North bids_____; East passes; South bids_____; All Pass. What is the contract_____? Who is the declarer_____? Who leads the first card_____? What is the lead_____?

#2   North

                      ♠1065

                      ♥KJ3

                      ♦KJ6

                      ♣10865

West   East

♠743   ♠QJ82

♥84   ♥10762

♦10983   ♦Q72

♣J974   ♣A3

                    South (Dealer)

                    ♠AK9

                    ♥AQ95

                    ♦A54

                    ♣KQ2

South is the dealer and with _____points and bids _____; West passes; North with _____points bids_____; East passes; South bids_____; West passes; North bids_____; All Pass. What is the contract_____? Who is the declarer_____? Who leads the first card_____? What is the lead_____?

#3

North
♠Q942
♥K10643
♦AK
♣A7

West
♠5
♥752
♦Q10754
♣10983

East
♠63
♥AJ
♦J9632
♣6542

South (Dealer)
♠AKJ1087
♥Q98
♦8
♣KQJ

South is the dealer with _____points and bids____; West passes; North with ____points bids____; East passes; South bids____; West passes; North bids____; East passes; South bids____; West passes; North bids____; All Pass.
What is the contract____? Who is the declarer____? Who leads the first card____?
What is the lead____?

#4

North
♠AK32
♥J764
♦K1093
♣4

West
♠1098
♥32
♦J852
♣Q1076

East
♠654
♥Q95
♦74
♣KJ982

South (Dealer)
♠QJ7
♥AK108
♦AQ6
♣A53

South is the dealer with _____points and bids ____; West passes; North with ____points bids____; East passes; South bids____; West passes; North bids____; East passes; South bids____; West passes; North bids ____; All Pass.
What is the contract____? Who is the declarer____? Who leads the first card____?
What is the lead____?

#5

North
♠KJ73
♥AQ2
♦A10
♣AQ84

West (Dealer)
♠1062
♥K974
♦J8432
♣J

East
♠84
♥J108
♦9765
♣10763

South
♠AQ95
♥653
♦KQ
♣K952

West is the dealer and passes; North with ____points bids____; East passes; South with ____points bids____; West passes; North bids____; East passes; South bids____; West passes; North bids____; East passes; South bids____; All Pass.
What is the contract____? Who is the declarer____? Who leads the first card____?
What is the lead____?

#6

North
♠AJ63
♥J83
♦AKJ10
♣K3

West (Dealer)
♠10
♥K10976
♦Q752
♣962

East
♠975
♥Q5
♦863
♣QJ1084

South
♠KQ842
♥A42
♦94
♣A75

West is the dealer and passes; North with ____points bids____; East passes; South with ____points bids____ (transfer); West passes; North bids____; East passes; South bids____; West passes; North bids ____; East passes; South bids____; All Pass.
What is the contract____? Who is the declarer____? Who leads the first card____?
What is the lead____?

#7

North
♠KQ7
♥AQJ
♦AJ2
♣AJ82

West (Dealer)
♠106
♥9742
♦10843
♣Q64

East
♠8432
♥K1086
♦976
♣107

South
♠AJ95
♥53
♦KQ5
♣K953

West is the dealer and passes; North with ____points bids____; East passes;
South with ____points bids____; West passes; North bids____; East passes; South bids____;
West passes; North bids____; East passes; South bids____; West passes; North bids____; East
passes; South bids____; All Pass.
What is the contract____? Who is the declarer____? Who leads the first card____?
What is the lead____?

#8

North
♠J63
♥K10
♦AK852
♣A93

West
♠109
♥Q875
♦QJ10
♣8642

East
♠75
♥J9632
♦763
♣QJ10

South (Dealer)
♠AKQ842
♥A4
♦94
♣K75

South is the dealer with ____points and bids____; West passes; North with ____points
bids____; East passes; South with ____points bids____; West passes; North bids____; East
passes; South bids____; West passes; North bids ____; East passes; South bids____;
West passes; North bids____; All Pass.
What is the contract____? Who is the declarer____? Who leads the first card____?
What is the lead____?

Answers to practice hands on pages 69 - 72.

#1

North is the dealer with 22 points and bids 2♣; East passes; South with 13 points bids 2♦ (waiting); West passes; North bids 2NT; East passes; South bids 3♣ (Stayman); West passes: North bids 3♦; East passes; South bids 4NT; West passes; North bids 5♠ (three aces); East passes; South bids 5NT; West passes; North bids 6♦ (one king); East passes; South bids 6NT; All Pass.

North is the declarer in 6NT. East leads the ♦8.

#2

South is the dealer with 22 points and bids 2♣; West passes; North with 8 points bids 2♦ (waiting); East passes; South bids 2NT; West passes; North bids 3NT; All Pass.

South is the declarer in 3NT. West leads the ♦10.

#3

South is the dealer with 18 points and bids 1♠; West passes; North with 19 points (2 doubleton points with a ♠ fit) makes a forcing bid of 2♥; East passes; South jumps to 3♠ showing 17-18 points and six or more spades; West passes; North bids 4NT (Blackwood). **The last suit bid naturally is the agreed suit**. East passes; South bids 5♦ (one ace); West passes; North only missing one ace bids 6♠; All Pass.

 South is the declarer in 6♠. West leads the ♣10.

#4

South is the dealer with 20 points and bids 2NT; West passes; North with 11 points bids 3♣ (Stayman); East passes; South bids 3♥; West passes; North now with 13 points (two points for the singleton club with the heart fit) bids 4NT; East passes; South bids 5♠ (three aces); West passes; North bids 6♥; All Pass.

South is the declarer in 6♥. West leads the ♠10.

Although the partnership has all four aces, South has limited his hand to 20-21 points by his opening 2NT bid. A grand slam does not seem to be an option on this deal with a possible combined 34-point count.

#5

West is the dealer and passes; North with 20 points bids 2NT; East passes; South with 14 points bids 3♣ (Stayman); West passes; North bids 3♠; East passes; South bids 4NT (Blackwood); West passes; North bids 5♠; East passes; South bids 6♠; All Pass. North is the declarer at 6♠. East leads the ♥J.

- After drawing trumps, declarer must play the ♣A first from his hand, and noticing the drop of West's ♣J, follow up with the ♣Q, then play the ♣8 to finesse East's ♣10.

#6

West the dealer and passes; North with 16 points bids 1NT; East passes; South with 14 points bids 2♥ (Jacoby transfer); West passes; North now has 17 points (one point for the doubleton club with the spade fit). North bids 3♠ (super accept); East passes; South now with 15 points (one point for the doubleton diamond with the known spade fit) bids 4NT (Blackwood); West passes; North bids 5♥ (two aces); East passes; South bids 6♠; All Pass. North is the declarer at 6♠. East leads the ♠9.

- East makes a passive lead of the ♠9 with no other good lead.
- To make the slam, declarer must take two finesses in diamonds to pitch his two heart losers.

#7

West is the dealer and passes; North with 22 points bids 2♣; East passes; South bids 2♦ (waiting bid); West passes; North bids 2NT; East passes; South bids 3♣ (Stayman); West passes; North bids 3♦; East passes; South bids 4NT (Blackwood); West passes; North bids 5♠ (three aces); East passes; South bids 6NT; All Pass.

North is the declarer at 6NT. East leads the ♠4.

- Not wanting to lead away from his ♥K, East makes a passive lead of the ♠4.

#8

South is the dealer with 18 points and bids 1♠; West passes; North with 17 points bids makes a forcing bid of 2♦; East passes; South jumps to 3♠; West passes; North bids a control bid of 4♣ **(spades is the last suit bid naturally and the presumed trump suit)**; East passes; South bids a control bid of 4♥ (by passing the diamond suit); West passes; North with the diamond suit under control bids 4NT (Blackwood); East passes; South bids 5♥ (two aces); West passes; North bids 6♠; All Pass.

South is the declarer at 6♠. West leads the ♦Q.

CHAPTER SIX   PREEMPTIVE BIDDING

A Preemptive Bid shows a Weak Hand with a Long Suit.

Two-Level Bids: six-card suit
Three-Level bids: seven-card suit
 Four-Level bids: eight-card suit (or 7-4 distribution)
 Five-Level bids: nine-card suit (or 8-4 distribution)

Suits headed by:
Two of the top three honors: AK, KQ, AQ or
Three of the top five honors Including the 10: KJ10, QJ10, AJ10

No more than 10 HCP: With 10 or less high card points, <u>do not</u> count for length when making a preemptive bid. With 11 or more high card points, count length and open on the one-level. You can preempt at the two, three, four and in some cases the five-level. You hand is borderline or too weak to open on the one-level in first, second or fourth seat. Preempts can successfully interfere with our opponents and can be fun and effective. However, preempts may involve some risks.

Vulnerability: When you preempt, you may be doubled for penalty and must consider the potential cost. A preempt is successful when you give up less than the contract your opponents could have made.

Positions:
 First and second seat: Your partner's hand is unknown.
   - **Your should have two of the top three honors, or three of the top five honors including the 10: AK, KQ, AQ, AQ10, AJ10, KJ10, and QJ10.**
   - Having good suit quality provides a safety net when preempting.
   - It's fine to have an ace or king outside of your preempt suit.
   - In second seat, you are preempting only one opponent and your partner, so your second seat preempts should be especially disciplined.

Third seat:
   - Partner is a passed hand, so game is remote.
   - Third seat preempts should have most of your strength in your long suit
   - You might preempt in third seat with less length or strength.

Fourth seat:
   - Preempts in fourth seat follow different guidelines.
   - Don't preempt two opponents who have not bid.
   - Open in fourth seat when you hope to make the contract.
   - Fourth suit preempts are never "weak" – they are often made with at least minimum opening values, which they would have opened as dealer on the one-level.

Preempt guidelines:
- **Vulnerable three-level preempts in first and second seat have most of their HCP in the preempt suit.**
- Holding trump support, raise with both weak and strong hands.
- Raise only non-forcing (RONF) can be seen on many convention cards.
- Do not bid 3NT after a three-level preempt **without a fit in partner's suit** so that you can reach his suit, or a long suit of your own that you can easily establish.
- Count your quick tricks when responding to a preempt.
- Fourth seat preempts should have close to an opening bid.
- Usually do not preempt in a minor or a major holding another decent four-card major.
- Normally, do not preempt holding a void or another five-card suit.

Example of competitive bidding: See scoring the game in Chapter 12.
- You will be especially eager to preempt if the opponents are **vulnerable** and may make their contract, and you are **non-vulnerable.**
- For example, an opponent will make 620 points for a vulnerable major suit game. If you are **non-vulnerable,** you can **afford** to go down three doubled for a minus 500 points if you determine the opponents' vulnerable game is making.

Weak Two Bids: We use an artificial 2♣ bid to show 22+ point hands or 8 ½ tricks. The 2♣ strong bid was devised so that 2♠, 2♥, or 2♦ can show weak two bids.
- **Weak two bids are opened with 6-10 HCP and a <u>six-card</u> suit headed by two of the top three honors, or three of the top five honors including the 10.**

Responses to weak two bids:
- Pass.
- Bid a new suit which is forcing.
- Bid a forcing 2NT.
- Raise the preempt suit to the three-level with three-card support to further the preempt. Raise the preempt suit to the four-level with four-card support with strong or weak hands to further the preempt.

Pass: Count quick tricks.
- Partner opens a preempt and promises 5-6 tricks in the suit. Count the number of **quick tricks** in your hand, and the tricks partner has promised to determine how high you will bid.

Example: Opener bids 2♥. Responder holds: ♠KQ8, ♥98, ♦KJ63, ♣KQ76
Responder's hand looks very good with all the kings and queens, and there maybe a 3NT or four-level major contract. However, count your quick tricks before bidding 2NT or four hearts.
You only have 2 ½ quick tricks (QT) and only two hearts.
♠KQ-1; ♥- 0; ♦KJ- ½, ♣KQ-1 = 2 ½ QT. Your 2 ½ QT plus partner's 5-6 tricks = 8-8 ½ tricks. <u>Pass the weak two bid, and hope to make it.</u>

Bid a New Suit: Forcing bid:
A new suit by responder is forcing for one round of bidding*:

- Opener preempts and responder holds a good six card major.
  Example of responder's suit: ♠AQJ1064 and 15+points.
- Responder's suit may be as good as the preempt suit.
- Preemptor may support partner's suit with three cards in partner's suit, or with no support for partner's suit, merely rebid the preempt suit.
- Preemptor with a solid suit AKQxxx may respond 3NT.

(*A new suit may be **non-forcing** with partnership agreement and would be **alertable).**

Raise preempt suit to game: **Raise preempt suit to game with four quick tricks.**

Example: Partner opens 2♠. Responder: ♠Q76, ♥AK42, ♦AK104, ♣32 = four QT
Partner's six tricks + your four quick tricks = ten tricks. Bid 4♠.

Forcing 2NT bid:

- A common strong response to a weak two bid is a forcing **2NT** by responder.
- Responder bids 2NT, asking weak two opener for a **"feature"** of an outside **ace or king.** The feature of the side suit a**ce or king** may be a necessary entry to the dummy hand if the partnership decides to play the contract in 3NT.
- The preemptor bids the feature, or merely rebids the preempt suit with no outside feature.

Further the preempt with strong or weak hands: Raise only non-forcing.

- **The "law of total tricks" indicates you can compete to the level of your combined trump fit. The partner of the preemptor can "further the preempt".**
- Responder with three cards in support of opener's preempt, and less than an opening hand, can raise to the three-level to further the preempt. The raise **is not an invitation to game and is non-forcing.**
- Responder with four cards in support of opener's preempt, and less than four quick tricks (especially non-vulnerable), can raise partner to game. Follow the "law of total tricks" when preempting with either strong (four quick tricks) or weak hands. Compete for as many tricks as the number of your combined trump length. Consider a higher point count range when vulnerable.

<u>Defending preempts:</u>

- Overcall with a strong five+card suit and opening values or better.
- A jump overcall shows a six+card suit with 14-16 points. Your bid is strong, not weak.
- Pass with your own preemptive bid. Don't preempt a preempt.
- Make a takeout double with shortness in preempt suit and opening values. You may have slightly less in balancing seat.
- Doubles of preempts through 4♥ are usually for takeout. A double of a 4♠ preempt is for takeout or penalty by partnership agreement.
- Bid 2NT with 16-18 points, and 3NT with 19+points and stoppers in the preempt suit

Preempt, pass or open one of a suit?

Answers at bottom of page

#1
♠KQJ10976
♥2
♦763
♣52
HCP____; Bid____

#2
♠8
♥AQJ876
♦984
♣1098
HCP____; Bid____

#3
♠AKJ10987
♥1076
♦54
♣4
HCP____; Bid____

#4
♠432
♥AKQJ109
♦J87
♣8
HCP____; Bid____

#5
♠42
♥92
♦AK10987
♣J96
HCP____; Bid____

#6
♠108
♥432
♦Q
♣KJ105432
HCP____; Bid____

#7
♠AK10932
♥1094
♦753
♣2
HCP____; Bid____

#8
♠963
♥K109876
♦Q72
♣6
HCP____; Bid____

#9
♠1098
♥AQJ1098
♦54
♣42
HCP____; Bid____

#10
♠K95432
♥J109
♦2
♣K102
HCP____; Bid____

#11
♠KJ8
♥Q4
♦J865432
♣Q
HCP____; Bid____

#12
♠KQJ8743
♥2
♦KQJ
♣76
HCP____; Bid____

#13
♠---
♥85
♦AQJ108432
♣1065
HCP____; Bid____

#14
♠---
♥85
♦K985432
♣10985
HCP____; Bid____

#15
♠8
♥98
♦Q75
♣AKQ10876
HCP____; Bid____

Answers:

HCP	BID		HCP	BID		HCP	BID
#1 6	3♠		#2 7	2♥		#3 8	3♠
#4 11	1♥		#5 8	2♦		#6 6	3♣
#7 7	2♠		#8 5	pass		#9 7	2♥
#10 7	pass		#11 9	pass		#12 12	4♠
#13 7	4♦		#14 3	pass		#15 11	1♣

78

CHAPTER SIX
THE BOTTOM LINE

A Preemptive Bid shows a Weak Hand with a Long Suit.

Two-Level Bids: six-card suit
Three-Level bids: seven-card suit
 Four-Level bids: eight-card suit (or 7-4 distribution)
 Five-Level bids: nine-card suit (or 8-4 distribution)

Suits headed by:
Two of the top three honors: AK, KQ, AQ or
Three of the top five honors Including the 10: KJ10, QJ10, AJ10

No More Than 6-10 HCP: With fewer than 10 points, do not count for length when making a preemptive bid. With 11 or more points, count length and open on the one-level.

Responses to weak two bids:

Pass:
* **Partner is promising 5-6 tricks in the preempt suit.** Pass with less than four quick tricks, and no support for preempt suit.

Bid a new suit: Forcing bid
* Responder holds a good six-card major suit, and at least **opening values.**
* Responder's suit may be as good as the preempt suit
* **Responder's new suit is forcing for one round of bidding.**

Raise preempt suit to game: Count winning tricks
* Partner's preempt bid promises five to six tricks in the preempt suit. With a fit in the suit and four quick tricks, raise to game vulnerable or non-vulnerable.

Forcing 2NT bid:
* Responder bids 2NT, asking partner for an outside "feature" of an ace or king in a suit other than the preempt suit. Responder is looking for an outside entry in preemptor's hand to play the contract in 3NT.
* A preemptive opener bids the feature, or merely rebids the preempt suit with no outside feature.

Further the preempt with strong or weak hands - non-forcing:
* Responder with three cards in support of opener's preempt, and less than an opening hand, can raise partner to the three-level to further the preempt. **The raise is not an invitation to game and is non-forcing.** Responder with four cards in support of partner's preempt, and with strong or weak hands, can raise partner to game. Compete to the level of your combined trump length according to the "law of total tricks" to further the preempt. Consider a higher point count range when vulnerable.

Practice hands: **Answers on page 83.**

#1   North (Dealer)
                           ♠8
                           ♥KQJ987
                           ♦QJ94
                           ♣106

West   East
♠KJ976   ♠Q543
♥A4   ♥103
♦872   ♦K53
♣QJ7   ♣9854

                           South
                           ♠A102
                           ♥652
                           ♦A106
                           ♣AK32

North is the dealer with ____points and bids____; East passes; South bids with ___points bids____; All Pass. What is the contract____? Who is the declarer____? Who leads the first card____? What is the lead____?

#2   North
                           ♠86
                           ♥KQ5
                           ♦Q642
                           ♣AKQJ

West   East
♠104   ♠Q7
♥J9763   ♥A1042
♦AK9   ♦J753
♣742   ♣953

                           South (Dealer)
                           ♠AKJ9532
                           ♥8
                           ♦108
                           ♣1086

South is the dealer with ____points and bids ____; West passes; North with ____points bids ____; All Pass. What is the contract____? Who is the declarer____? Who leads the first card____? What is the lead ____?

#3

North
♠102
♥K1082
♦J64
♣QJ98

West (Dealer)
♠AQ9863
♥4
♦K53
♣643

East
♠K54
♥973
♦A987
♣A102

South
♠J7
♥AQJ65
♦Q102
♣K75

West is the dealer with ___points and bids____; North passes; East bids___; All Pass.
What is the contract____? Who is the declarer____? Who leads the first card____?
What is the lead____?

#4

North
♠1062
♥K10943
♦AJ
♣Q65

West
♠Q98
♥AQJ
♦10876432
♣ ---

East
♠AK754
♥8765
♦Q5
♣K2

South (Dealer)
♠J3
♥2
♦K9
♣AJ1098743

South is the dealer with ___point and bids____; All Pass.
What is the contract____? Who is the declarer____? Who leads the first card____?
What is the lead____?

#5

North

♠K8
♥65
♦K832
♣Q7532

West

♠J654
♥A42
♦A5
♣J984

East

♠AQ97
♥93
♦QJ97
♣K63

South (Dealer)

♠1032
♥KQJ1087
♦106
♣A10

South is the dealer with ___points and bids____; West passes; North passes; East makes a takeout double, South passes; West ____; All Pass.
What is the contract____? Who is the declarer____? Who leads the first card____?
What is the lead____?

#6

North (Dealer)

♠8
♥KQ8
♦32
♣QJ109872

West

♠J973
♥A94
♦J984
♣53

East

♠AK642
♥J10762
♦105
♣4

South

♠Q105
♥53
♦AKQ76
♣AK6

North is the dealer with ___point and bids____; East passes; South with ____points bids____ (forcing); West passes; North bids____; East passes; South bids____; All Pass.
What is the contract____? Who is the declarer____? Who leads the first card____?
What is the lead____?

Answers for preempt hands on pages 80 - 82.

#1

North is the dealer with 9 HCP and bids 2♥; East passes; South with 16 points and four quick tricks bids 4♥; All Pass.
North is declarer in 4♥. East leads the ♠3.

#2

South is the dealer with 9 HCP and bids 3♠; West passes; North with four quick tricks and spade support bids 4♠; All Pass.
South is the declarer in 4♠. West leads the ♦A.

#3

West is the dealer with 9 HCP and bids 2♠; North passes; East bids 3♠ (furthers the preempt); All Pass.
West is the declarer in 3♠. North leads the ♣Q.

#4

South is the dealer with 9 HCP and bids 4♣; All Pass.
South is the declarer in 4♣. West leads the ♦10.

#5

South is the dealer with 10 HCP and bids 2♥; West passes; North passes; East makes a takeout double; South passes; West bids 2♠; All Pass.

West is the declarer in 2♠; North leads 6♥, top of a doubleton in partner's suit.

#6

North is the dealer with 8 HCP and bids 3♣; East passes; South with 19 points bids 3♦ (forcing); West passes; North bids 3♥ (feature); East passes; South bids 5♣; All Pass.
North is the declarer in 5♣. East leads the ♠A.

NOTES

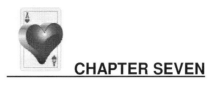

 **OVERCALLS**   **TAKEOUT DOUBLES**

OVERCALLS:

When your RHO opens the bidding, it is important to overcall with a good five+card suit to compete with the opponents. If you are a weak overcall, you may be outbid so your suit should be good enough for partner to lead your suit. Overcalls are usually made in direct seat, immediately over your RHO's opening bid. An overcall in the fourth seat after two passes is called a **"balancing"** overcall. **A one-level overcall does not promise or deny an opening bid.**

Why Overcall?

- When you overcall, you've introduced a suit which may act as a lead director for partner if the opponents win the contract.
- You may push the opponents too high, or you may find a part score.
- You also may want to make a **"sacrifice"** bid. A sacrifice is a competitive bid that may not be successful, however, your sacrifice bid may be less costly than allowing the opponents to make their contract especially if they are vulnerable and you are non-vulnerable.

OVERCALL REQUIREMENTS:

8-16 points: overcalls at the one-level.
12-16 points: overcalls at the two-level.
17+points: double then bid a new suit, jump in partner's suit or bid notrump.

- **Overcall your RHO's opening bid with a good five+card suit. Don't overcall with a four-card suit unless the suit includes at least three or four top honors.**
- Overcalls at the one-level may have less than an opening hand and a five+card suit.
- Overcalls at the two-level require an opening hand of 12-16 points, and a five+card suit.
- Your one-level overcall does not deny an opening bid.
- Consider not overcalling with 17+points. You may make a Big Hand takeout double first, then change suits, jump in partner's suit. or bid notrump with stoppers in the opponent's suit.
- A 2NT overcall of a weak two bid is a balanced hand with 15-18 points, and at least one stopper in the opponent's suit.
- A balanced overcall hand with 18-20 points and stoppers in the opener's suit, should double first to show strength, and then bid no-trump, while a hand with 21-22 should double and then jump in no-trump.

Responses to partner's overcalls:

With support:

- Raise partner's suit at the two-level with three support cards and 6-10 points.
- Non-vulnerable, four support cards and 10 or less points, make a preemptive jump to the three-level using the law of total tricks, partnership agreement.
- Non-vulnerable, five support cards and 10 or less points, make a preemptive jump to the four-level using the law of total tricks, partnership agreement.
- Or may bid a limit raise at the three-level with 11-14 points, partnership agreement.
- Respond to two-level overcalls as if partner made an opening bid with 12-16 points and a five-card suit. Raise to game with 15-16 points.

Without support:

- New suit responses to one-level overcalls are non-forcing but encouraging.
- New suits by responder to two-level overcalls are forcing, unless by a passed hand.
- Respond to two-level overcalls as if partner made an opening bid with 12-16 points and a five-card suit.
- With no support for partner's <u>one-level overcall</u> suit and 17+points, the only forcing bid is a "cue bid" in the opponent's opening suit. The cue bid of the opener's suit is artificial and forcing overcaller to bid again.

Responses to partner's overcalls <u>**with support**</u>.

<u>One-level overcalls:</u>
6-10 points: Raise at the two-level.
6-10 points: Preemptive jump at the three-level, vulnerability a factor.
6-10 points: Preemptive jump at the four-level, vulnerability a factor.
11-14 points: Jump at the three-level, limit raise, partnership agreement.
15-16 points: Raise to game level.

<u>Two-level overcalls:</u>
8-11 points: Raise to the three-level.
12-16 points: Bid game.
17+points: Cuebid opponent's suit.

Responses to partner's overcalls <u>*without* **support**</u>.

<u>One-level overcalls</u>:
8-12 points: Bid a new suit at the one-level with good 5-card suit.
13-16 points: Jump in new suit with a good 5-card suit.
17+points: Cuebid opponent's suit

<u>Two-level overcalls:</u>
10+points: Bid new suit, forcing.
10-12 points: Bid 2NT with stoppers in opponent's suit.
13-16 points: Bid 3NT with stoppers in opponent's suit.
17+points: Bid new suit forcing, then explore for slam.

Sample overcall hand:

Contract: 4♠   East leads the ♥A

Bidding:

West	North	East	South
1♥	1♠ (overcall)	2♥	3♠
Pass	4♠	All Pass	

```
                        North
                        ♠KQ1042
                        ♥654
                        ♦KQ4
                        ♣74
    West (Dealer)                              East
    ♠63                                        ♠97
    ♥KQJ1042                                   ♥A873
    ♦A105                                      ♦J76
    ♣K2                                        ♣10985
                        South
                        ♠AJ85
                        ♥9
                        ♦9832
                        ♣AQJ6
```

Declarer makes a game plan after the seeing the opening lead and the dummy. Declarer has one or two diamond losers, a possible club loser and three heart losers. Declarer plans to trump his heart losers in the dummy before drawing opponent's trumps. Declarer will finesse West's ♦A by leading toward the ♦KQ in his hand, and take the ♣K finesse.

- East leads the ♥A, declarer plays dummy's ♥9, West the ♥2, North follows with the ♥4. East can see that there are no more hearts in the dummy, and switches to the ♠9 to shorten dummy's trumps to prevent heart ruffs in dummy. Declarer wins the trick with the ♠A. Declarer plays a low diamond from dummy (playing low or up to an honor). West plays a low diamond, North plays the ♦K. As the ♦K won the trick, declarer presumes West has the ♦A. Declarer trumps a losing heart in dummy, the short side of the trump suit.

- Declarer now plays a diamond toward the ♦Q in his hand. West may now decide to play the ♦A, and lead a second trump to shorten dummy's trumps for declarer's heart ruffs.

- Declarer wins the trump lead in his hand, and trumps his last losing heart in dummy. Declarer draws opponent's last trump. Declarer plays a low club to the ♣Q in the dummy losing to the ♣K. Declarer loses a heart, diamond and club and making the 4♠ contract.

Weak Jump Overcalls: Preemptive Bids

- A jump overcall in a new suit over your RHO opening bid is preemptive, and shows a weak hand and a long suit.
- You can make a weak jump overcall at the two-level, three-level or four-level with 6-10 HCP. Length points are not counted.
- Weak jump overcalls suggests two of the top three honors, or three of the top five honors including the 10, especially when vulnerable.

Two-level jump overcalls: six-card suit - weak two bid
Three-level jump overcalls: seven-card suit - weak three bid
Four-level jump overcalls: eight-card suit - weak four bid

Sample jump overcall hand:

Contract: 3♠   West leads the ♥4.
Bidding:

East (Dealer)	South (jump overcall)	West	North
1♥	2♠	3♥	3♠
All Pass			

North
♠J64
♥K10
♦8432
♣KQ75

West
♠75
♥J85**4**
♦QJ6
♣AJ62

East (Dealer)
♠K8
♥AQ632
♦A975
♣83

South
♠AQ10932
♥97
♦K10
♣1094

- East is the dealer with 14 points and opens the bidding 1♥.
- South with 9 HCP makes a weak jump 2♠ overcall.
- West competes to 3♥ with 10 points and four trumps (one point for the doubleton spade).
- North furthers the spade preempt to 3♠ knowing there is a nine-card spade fit. All Pass.
- South's weak jump overcall prevented a 3♥ part score by East-West, and resulted in making a 3♠ contract.

Notrump Overcalls: Contract: 3NT   West leads the ♠5

East	South	West	North
1♠	1NT (overcall)	Pass	2♣ (Stayman)
Pass	2♦	Pass	3NT
All Pass			

North
♠96
♥QJ108
♦J932
♣AQ10

West
♠87**5**
♥932
♦7654
♣983

East (Dealer)
♠KJ1043
♥A653
♦K8
♣K4

South (1NT overcaller)
♠AQ2
♥K74
♦AQ10
♣J762

- East is the dealer with 15 points and opens the bidding 1♠.

- **South overcalls 1NT.**

- **South must have spade stoppers and 15 -18 points for the 1NT overcall of the spade suit. South has the ♠AQ well placed behind the 1♠ opening bid.**

Systems of Stayman and Jacoby transfers are "on" over a 1NT overcall.

- North bids Stayman with 10 points and a four-card heart suit.

- South bids 2♦ denying a four-card major.

- North with 10 points bids 3NT.

In the play declarer knocks out the ♥A and takes the diamond finesse by leading the ♦J and letting it run for nine tricks, with two spades, three hearts, three diamonds and one club.

Responses to partner's overcalls **with support**.

One-level overcalls:
6-10 points: Raise at the two-level.
6-10 points: Preemptive jump at the three-level, vulnerability a factor.
6-10 points: Preemptive jump at the four-level, vulnerability a factor.
11-14 points: Jump at the three-level, limit raise, partnership agreement.
15-16 points: Raise to game level.

Two-level overcalls:
8-11 points: Raise to the three-level.
12-16 points: Bid game.
17+points: Cuebid opponent's suit.

Responses to partner's overcalls *without* support.

One-level overcalls:
8-12 points: Bid a new suit at the one-level with good 5-card suit.
13-16 points: Jump in new suit with a good 5-card suit.
17+points: Cuebid opponent's suit

Two-level overcalls:
10+points: Bid new suit, forcing.
10-12 points: Bid 2NT with stoppers in opponent's suit.
13-16 points: Bid 3NT with stoppers in opponent's suit.
17+points: Bid new suit forcing, then explore for slam.

Weak Jump Overcalls:

- A weak jump overcall in a new suit over an opponent's opening bid is preemptive, and shows a weak hand, a six+card suit, and no more than 10 HCP. Length points are not counted.

Notrump Overcalls:

- Hands with 15-18 points and **stoppers in an opponent's opening suit,** can overcall 1NT.
- All systems are in place such as Stayman and Jacoby transfers.

#1

North
♠Q652
♥J98
♦J1098
♣K6

West
♠98
♥AQ1054
♦AQ3
♣832

East
♠74
♥K763
♦K72
♣A1095

South (Dealer)
♠AKJ103
♥2
♦654
♣QJ74

South is the dealer with _____points and bids____; West with ____points overcalls ____;
North with ____ points bids____; East with ____points bids____; All Pass.
What is the contract____? Who is the declarer____? Who leads the first card____?
What is the lead____?

#2

North
♠K54
♥K86
♦J53
♣7643

West
♠Q1083
♥543
♦Q76
♣952

East
♠AJ762
♥J7
♦K104
♣AJ10

South (Dealer)
♠9
♥AQ1092
♦A982
♣KQ8

South is the dealer with ____points and bids ____; West passes; North with ____points
bids____; East with____ points bids____; South bids____; West passes; North bids____;
All Pass. What is the contract____? Who is the declarer____? Who leads the first card____?
What is the lead____?

#3   North (Dealer)
                                      ♠42
                                      ♥AQ1063
                                      ♦10
                                      ♣AJ763

West   East
♠Q1095   ♠AKJ87
♥J   ♥742
♦AQ953   ♦J72
♣KQ8   ♣109

                                      South
                                      ♠63
                                      ♥K985
                                      ♦K864
                                      ♣542

North is the dealer with _____points and bids____; East overcalls____; South bids____; West now with ____points bids____; North passes; East bids____; All Pass.
What is the contract____? Who is the declarer____? Who leads the first card____?
What is the lead____?

#4   North
                                      ♠A9
                                      ♥A76
                                      ♦108543
                                      ♣Q65

West (Dealer)   East
♠Q654   ♠KJ1032
♥10   ♥82
♦KQ2   ♦J76
♣AKJ87   ♣1092

                                      South
                                      ♠87
                                      ♥KQJ9543
                                      ♦A9
                                      ♣43

West is the dealer with ____points and bids____; North passes; East with ____points bids____; South bids____; West bids____; All Pass. What is the contract____? Who is the declarer____? Who leads the first card____? What is the lead____?

#5

North
♠KJ10874
♥KJ4
♦109
♣K4

West (Dealer)
♠63
♥92
♦AKQ875
♣Q108

East
♠9
♥10753
♦J643
♣A962

South
♠AQ52
♥AQ86
♦2
♣J753

West is the dealer with _____points and bids____; North with ____points overcalls ____;
East bids____; South with ____points bids____; West passes; North bids____; All Pass.
What is the contract____? Who is the declarer____? Who leads the first card____?
What is the lead____?

#6

North
♠9
♥AKJ54
♦975
♣Q982

West (Dealer)
♠AKQJ76
♥63
♦K102
♣K10

East
♠8432
♥Q109
♦Q8
♣AJ53

South
♠105
♥872
♦AJ643
♣764

West is the dealer with _____points and bids____; North with ____points overcalls ____;
East with ____points bids____; South passes; West bids____; All Pass.
What is the contract____? Who is the declarer____? Who leads the first card____?
What is the lead____?

#7

North
♠KJ7
♥K532
♦AK6
♣QJ3

West (Dealer)
♠A9842
♥64
♦J102
♣AK2

East
♠65
♥J7
♦Q9853
♣7654

South
♠Q103
♥AQ1098
♦74
♣1098

West is the dealer with _____points and bids ____; North with ____points overcalls____;
East passes; South with _____points bids_____; North announces TRANSER; West passes;
North SUPER ACCEPTS the transfer and bids____; East passes; South now with ____points
bids____; All Pass. What is the contract____? Who is the declarer____? Who leads the first
card____? What is the lead____?

#8

North
♠J653
♥8632
♦K109
♣A4

West
♠K92
♥Q1095
♦A64
♣875

East (Dealer)
♠8
♥AKJ74
♦QJ87
♣QJ6

South
♠AQ1074
♥---
♦532
♣K10932

East is the dealer with ____points and bids___; South overcalls ____; West with ____points
bids____; North with ____bids ____; East bids____; All Pass. What is the contract____?
Who is the declarer____? Who leads the first card____? What is the lead____?

Answers to practice hands pages 91 - 94.

#1

South is the dealer with 12 points and bids 1♠; West with 13 points overcalls 2♥; North With 7 points bids 2♠; East with 11 points (one point for the doubleton spade) bids 3♥; All Pass. West is declarer in 3♥. North leads the ♠5.

#2

South is the dealer with 16 points and bids 1♥; West passes; North with 7 points bids 2♥; East with 15 points overcalls 2♠; South bids 3♦ (help suit try); West passes; All Pass. South is the declarer in 3♥. West leads the ♠3.

#3

North is the dealer with 13 points and bids 1♥; East with 10 points overcalls 1♠; South with 7 points bids 2♥; West now with 16 points jumps to 4♠; All Pass. East is the declarer in 4♠. South leads the ♥5.

#4

West is the dealer with 16 points and bids 1♣; North passes; East with 6 points bids 1♠; South with 12 points overcalls 2♥; West now with 18 points (two points for the singleton heart) jumps to 3♠; All Pass.
East is the declarer in 3♠. South leads the ♥K.

#5

West is the dealer with 13 points and bids 1♦; North with 13 points overcalls 1♠; East bids 2♦; South bids 3♠; West passes; North bids 4♠; All Pass.
North is the declarer in 4♠. East leads the ♦3.

#6

West is the dealer with 18 points and bids 1♠; North with 13 points overcalls 2♥ (adding two points for the singleton spade. Although there is no suit agreement, the singleton in your RHO suit is valuable) East with 9 points bids 2♠; South passes; West now with 19 points bids 4♠; (one point for the doubleton heart); All Pass. West is the declarer in 4♠. North leads the ♥A.

#7

West is the dealer with 13 points and bids 1♠; North with 17 points overcalls 1NT; East passes; South with 9 points bids 2♦ - Jacoby transfer to hearts; North announces the transfer; West passes; North super accepts the transfer and jumps to 3♥; East passes; South now with 10 points (one point for the doubleton diamond) bids 4♥; All Pass. North is the declarer in 4♥. East leads the ♠6.

#8

East is the dealer with 15 points and bids 1♥; South overcalls 1♠; West bids 2♥; North bids 2♠; East bids 3♥; All Pass. East is the declarer in 3♥. South leads the ♣3.

NOTES

 **TAKEOUT DOUBLES:**

In the past, any doubles made in the bidding were considered penalty doubles. One of the uses for a double in modern bidding is a request for **takeout** after the opponents have opened the bidding or agreed a suit.

A takeout double asks partner to bid his best suit.

- When your RHO opens the bidding, your takeout double asks partner to bid his best suit, or notrump with stoppers in the opponent's opening suit. Your takeout double is never a penalty double at low levels. When not in direct seat, takeout doubles can also be made to show suits not bid by the opponents.

Two types of takeout doubles:

- Ordinary takeout double: 12-16 points. Shortness in RHO's suit.
- "Big Hand" takeout double: 17+points. Any distributional shape is unsuitable for an overcall of 1NT.

The ordinary takeout double: An opening hand with 12-16 points.

- Your takeout double shows you have an opening hand, and can support any suit partner bids. You usually suggest the other four-card major if your RHO opens a major.

- You typically don't have a good five+card suit, or you might overcall RHO's opening bid rather than double.

- You may **count extra points for short suits** in your RHO's suit **before** hearing a fit with partner. You are counting on a presumed fit with partner, which is called dummy points**.**

Example: RHO opens 1♥. Make a takeout double with the following hand.
♠KQ98, ♥5, ♦KJ76, ♣Q1054 - **11 HCP+2 points for the singleton heart = 13 points.**

In the above example, you are short in your RHO suit, and you don't have a five+card suit to overcall. **Make a takeout double**.

Don't make an "off shape" takeout double holding three+cards in RHO's suit.

- In the ordinary takeout double, holding too many cards in RHO's opening suit may lead you to having insufficient cards in your other three suits to support partner's suit. You also may have too many losers in the opponent's suit.

Example: RHO opens 1♣: You hold: ♠A3 ♥Q74 ♦KQ96 ♣Q872.
With no other bid, you must **pass**. You hope partner makes a re-opening double, or bids a suit you can support later in the auction.

Responses to takeout doubles when responder's RHO bids.

Suit bids:

6+points: Bid four+card major not bid by LHO.

6+points: Bid a new suit at the one-level, or if necessary at the two-level.

10+points: Jump in a new suit at the two-level or three-level.

Notrump bids:

6-10 points, balanced: Bid 1NT with stoppers in LHO suit.

11-12 points, balanced: Jump to 2NT with stoppers in LHO suit.

13-15 points, balanced: Jump to 3NT with stoppers in LHO suit.

Responses to takeout double when responder's RHO passes:

- When opener makes a takeout double and responder's RHO passes.
- Responder is forced to bid even with zero points.
- If responder passes, the auction will end allowing the opponents to make a one-level doubled contract.

Respond with the following guidelines.

Responder is forced to bid:

0-8 points: Bid suit at the one-level (or if necessary, at the two-level).

9-11 points: Jump a level in your suit.

12+points: Cue bid the opponent's opening suit, or jump to game in a major.

Example of cue bid: LHO bids 1♥; partner makes a takeout double, and your RHO Passes. Cue bid 2♥ to show 12+points and at least strong invitational values*.

*You may also pass to convert the takeout double to a penalty double holding at least five+cards and honors in LHO's opening suit.

Sample ordinary takeout double hand:

Contract: 4♥   East leads ♠A
Bidding:

East (Dealer)	South	West	North
1♠	Double	Pass	3♥ (9-11 points)
Pass	4♥	All Pass	

North (Declarer)
♠1064
♥AQ83
♦72
♣QJ98

West
♠Q9
♥542
♦10986
♣6542

East (Dealer)
♠**A**K8732
♥109
♦K54
♣A7

South
♠J5
♥KJ76
♦AQJ3
♣K103

East opens the bidding 1♠. South holds 15 points, adding one point for the doubleton spade as he is counting on dummy points when finding a fit in a suit from partner (do npt also count the ♠J as a point – only as a doubleton).

- **South makes a takeout double. West passes. North is forced to bid after West passes. North jumps to 3♥ to show 9-11 points(one point for the doubleton diamond) and a four+card heart suit. South bids 4♥.**

- East wins the ♠AK, and plays a third spade, ruffed in dummy with the ♥J, as West has shown a high-low play of the ♠Q and ♠9 indicating a doubleton spade. East was hoping West could over-ruff the dummy with this play of the third spade.

- A low club is led from dummy to the ♣9 in his declarer's hand, losing to East's ♣A.

- East plays back a club, declarer wins and draws trumps.

- Declarer takes the diamond finesse for 10 tricks.

THE "BIG HAND" TAKEOUT DOUBLE (BHTD):

- The BHTD shows a 17+point hand.
- The BHTD also asks partner to bid his best suit.
- However, the BHTD does not simply raise partner's suit on his rebid as in the ordinary takeout double.

At his second turn to bid, the Big Hand takeout doubler bids a new suit, jumps in partner's suit with 17-18 points, or with 19-21 points, jump shifts in a new suit or bids notrump with stoppers in the opponent's suit.

- With 17+points, double first, as a simple overcall may not show the strength of your hand.
- The BHTD may have any distribution in addition to the 17+points.
- By changing suits or jumping in responder's suit, you show the BHTD and your 17-18 point count.
- Even a raise in a non-competitive auction shows real extras (15-17).
- You can also jump shift at your second turn to show an even stronger 19-21 point count.

Sample hand: RHO bids 1♥. You hold 19 points with: ♠AK10987, ♥K7, ♦AK102, ♣2

- In the sample hand, make a takeout double first, and then jump shift in the spade suit if responder bids a different suit.
- The jump shift in the new suit shows 19+points. Even doubling and then bidding spades at the minimum level would show real extras.
- If partner bids spades, you can jumps in spades after a non-jump bid from responder, or bid game in spades if partner shows 9-11 points.

Until responder hears opener's rebid showing the BHTD, responder will bid according to ordinary takeout double responses which are repeated below. Upon hearing a change of suits, or a jump or jump shift, responder will bid according to his point count and distribution.

Notrump bids:

6-10 points, balanced: Bid 1NT with stoppers in LHO suit.
11-12 points, balanced: Jump to 2NT with stoppers in LHO suit.
13-15 points, balanced: Jump to 3NT with stoppers in LHO suit.

Notrump bids:

6-10 points, balanced: Bid 1NT with stoppers in LHO suit.
11-12 points, balanced: Jump to 2NT with stoppers in LHO suit.
13-15 points, balanced: Jump to 3NT with stoppers in LHO suit.

Responder is forced to bid:

0-8 points: Bid suit at the one-level (or if necessary, at the two-level).
9-11 points: Jump a level in your suit.
12+points: Cue bid the opponent's opening suit, or jump to game in a major. You may also pass to convert the takeout double to a penalty double holding at least five+cards and honors in LHO's opening suit.

Sample BHTD hand:

Contract: 5♦   West leads ♠3

Bidding:

East (Dealer)	South	West	North
1♠	Double	Pass	3♥ (9-11 points)
Pass	4♦	Pass	5♦
All Pass			

```
                          North
                          ♠10
                          ♥AJ743
                          ♦10932
                          ♣Q53

West                                          East (Dealer)
♠Q963                                         ♠AK872
♥852                                          ♥Q96
♦J4                                           ♦65
♣8642                                         ♣AJ73
                          South
                          ♠J5
                          ♥K10
                          ♦AKQ876
                          ♣K109
```

- East opens the bidding 1♠.
- South holds 18 points.
- South does not want to merely overcall 2♦, planning to double first, and rebid the diamond suit after hearing any bid from partner.
- West passes.
- **North is forced to bid after West passes. North jumps to 3♥ to show 9-11 points (two points for the singleton spade) and a four+card heart suit.**
- South bids 4♦, change of suit, showing 17+points and a diamond suit.
- North adds South 17+points with his 10 points and bids the 5♦ game.

After drawing opponent's trumps in two rounds, South leaves the ♦10 in dummy as an entry to dummy's heart suit. South plays two rounds of hearts, and trumps the third round setting up the heart suit in dummy for a club sluff.

South will lose one spade and one club to make the 5♦ contract.

CHAPTER SEVEN
THE BOTTOM LINE

TAKEOUT DOUBLES

TWO TYPES OF TAKEOUT DOUBLES:

Ordinary Takeout Double: 12-16 points and shortness in RHO's suit.

- RHO opens the bidding. Your takeout double shows 12-16 points, shortness in RHO opening suit, and asks partner to bid his best suit.
- Do not make an "off shape" takeout double holding three+cards in RHO's suit unless you have more than a minimum opener.

Big Hand Takeout Double: 17+ points, any distribution.

- "Big Hand" takeout double: 17+points. Any distributional shape is unsuitable for an overcall of 1NT.
- Holding 17-18 points, the BHTD rebids a new suit, jumps in partner's suit.
- Holding 19-21 points, jump shifts in a new suit, bids game in partner's suit, or bids notrump with stoppers in the opponent's suit.

Responses for all takeout doubles:

Notrump bids:
6-10 points, balanced: Bid 1NT with stoppers in LHO suit.
11-12 points, balanced: Jump to 2NT with stoppers in LHO suit.
13-15 points, balanced: Jump to 3NT with stoppers in LHO suit.

Notrump bids:
6-10 points, balanced: Bid 1NT with stoppers in LHO suit.
11-12 points, balanced: Jump to 2NT with stoppers in LHO suit.
13-15 points, balanced: Jump to 3NT with stoppers in LHO suit.

Responder is forced to bid:
0-8 points: Bid suit at the one-level (or if necessary, at the two-level).
9-11 points: Jump a level in your suit.
12+points: Cue bid the opponent's opening suit, or jump to game in a major. You may also pass to convert the takeout double to a penalty double holding at least five+cards and honors in LHO's opening suit.

#1

North
- ♠642
- ♥1087
- ♦85432
- ♣87

West
- ♠KJ75
- ♥54
- ♦KQ10
- ♣A1065

East
- ♠AQ93
- ♥K92
- ♦J76
- ♣QJ3

South (Dealer)
- ♠108
- ♥AQJ63
- ♦A9
- ♣K942

South is the dealer with _____points and bids____; West bids with ____points makes a takeout double, North passes; East bids____; South passes; West bids____; North passes; East bids____; All Pass. What is the contract____? Who is the declarer____? Who leads the first card____? What is the lead____?

#2

North
- ♠764
- ♥Q108
- ♦J98
- ♣9864

West
- ♠AQ108
- ♥3
- ♦Q753
- ♣KQJ2

East
- ♠KJ32
- ♥542
- ♦K102
- ♣A53

South (Dealer)
- ♠95
- ♥AKJ976
- ♦A64
- ♣107

South is the dealer with _____points and bids____; West with ____points makes a takeout double; North passes; East with ____points bids____; South passes; West bids____; All Pass. What is the contract____? Who is the declarer____? Who leads the first card____? What is the lead____?

#3

North
♠Q954
♥J102
♦32
♣A752

West
♠1062
♥763
♦QJ105
♣J104

East (Dealer)
♠J73
♥A4
♦AK964
♣863

South
♠AK8
♥KQ985
♦87
♣KQ9

East is the dealer with _____points and bids ____; South with ____points makes a Big Hand takeout double; West passes; North bids____; East passes; South bids____; West passes; North bids____; All Pass. What is the contract____? Who is the declarer____? Who leads the first card____? What is the lead____?

#4

North
♠K976
♥K1052
♦109
♣743

West
♠54
♥J873
♦K54
♣10952

East (Dealer)
♠2
♥96
♦QJ832
♣AKQJ8

South
♠AQJ1083
♥AQ4
♦A76
♣6

East is the dealer with _____points and bids ____; South with ____points makes a Big Hand takeout double; West passes; North bids____; East passes; South bids____; West passes; North bids ____; All Pass.What is the contract____? Who is the declarer____? Who leads the first card____? What is the lead____?

Answers to practice hands from pages 103 - 104.

#1

South is the dealer with 15 points and bids 1♥; West with 14 points makes a takeout double, North passes; East bids 2♥ to show 12+points; South passes, West bids 2♠. North passes; East bids 4♠; All Pass.

West is the declarer in 4♠. North leads the ♥7.

#2

South is the dealer with 14 points and bids 1♥; West with 16 points (14 points + 2 points for the singleton heart); makes a takeout double; North passes; East with 11 points jumps to 2♠ (9-11) points; South passes; West bids 4♠; All Pass.

East is the declarer in 4♠. South leads the ♥A.

#3

East is the dealer with 13 points and bids 1♦; South with 19 points (one extra point for the doubleton diamond) makes a Big Hand takeout double; West passes; North bids 1♠; East passes; South jump shifts to 3♥; West passes; North bids 4♥; All Pass.

South is the declarer in 4♥. West leads the ♦Q.

#4

East is the dealer with 15 points and bids 1♣; South with 21 points (2 points for the singleton club) makes a Big Hand takeout double; West passes; North bids 1♥ showing 0-8 points, and bidding his major suits up-the-line; East passes; South jumps shifts to 3♠; North bids 4♠. All Pass.

South is the declarer in 4♠. West 2♣.

NOTES

 **CHAPTER EIGHT**

 THE BALANCING SEAT:

Balancing is defined as a reopening bid when the opponents' auction.
stops at a low level. You are in the <u>balancing seat</u> when your LHO opens one of a suit
followed by two passes. Your pass would end the auction.

<u>**A Good Rule of Thumb is to Add Three Points to Your Hand
When You Make a Balancing Bid**</u>.

**Balance with a good suit, bid notrump or double.
Use the higher range of your
balancing point count requirements when vulnerable**.

Example:
LHO bids 1♠   Partner-Passes   RHO-Passes
- You are in the balancing fourth seat with: ♠987, ♥AQ1054, ♦QJ3, ♣108 - Bid 2♥
- You would be too weak to overcall 2♥ in second seat - but here you can balance in fourth seat.

Example:
LHO bids 1♣   Partner-Passes   RHO-Passes
- Balancing seat with: ♠AJ32 ♥10965, ♦A984, ♣10 - balance with a takeout double.

Best time to balance:
- Partner may have been forced to pass when holding decent values but with length in opponent's suit.
- You are short in the opponent's suit.
- If you pass, opponents may make their bid at the one-level.
- You and your partner probably have half of the high card values available.
- If you defend, your bid will help your partner's choice of opening leads.
- You may also have a part score for a sacrifice when the opponents have a part score.
- You may push the opponents to a higher level of bidding, and turn their plus into a minus.

Do not balance:
- If your hand has less than 9 points, and no long suit or only a weak suit.
- You have length and/or strength in your LHO's opening suit.
- You are vulnerable and sub-minimum, when you must bid your suit at the two-level, which may lead to a double and costly penalty.

Over a one-level-bid of a suit by LHO: Balance with 9+points
- **9-14 points:** Balance with five+cards in a suit, and use the higher range of points if you make a two-level overcall.
- **12-14 points:** Bid 1NT with stoppers or length in opponent's suit.
- **15-17 points:** <u>Double, then bid 1NT with stoppers or length in opponent's suit.</u>
- **10+14 points:** Double for takeout with shortness in opponent's suit.
- **15+points:** Double for takeout then bid a **new suit** with five+cards in the suit.

Conventional bids:
- **9+points:** If your RHO bids a major, 2NT can be the unusual notrump conventional bid showing 5-5 in the minors.
  Also, a balancing cue bid of opener's suit can show a conventional Michaels two-suited hand.

Responses to partner's balancing seat bid: You need a somewhat higher range of points than if partner had overcalled in second seat.
- **9-11 points:** Raise partner's suit at the two-level.
- **12-16 points:** Jump raise of partner's suit invites game.
- **11+points:** Bid a new suit.
- **9-11 points:** Bid 1NT. As before, this suggests no fit for partner' suit, and stoppers in the opponents suit.
- **12-13 points:** Jump to 2NT with stoppers in the opponent's suit.
- **14-16 points:** Jump to 3NT with stoppers in the opponent's suit.

Sample balancing hands:

LHO bids 1♥ followed by two passes. You are in the balancing seat. What is your bid?

#1 ♠K4　　♥KQ2　　♦A1065　　♣Q1086　　14 points
Answer: Bid 1NT - 12-14 points. (With 15-17 points double first and then bid 1NT).

#2 ♠63　　♥J875　　♦KQ1065　　♣Q8　　9 points
Answer: Pass - You have a good suit but weak hand and length in opponent's heart suit.

#3 ♠K4　　♥86　　♦J108　　♣AJ10985　　11 points
Answer: Bid 2♣ - Bid your good suit with shortness in opponent's heart suit.

#4 ♠AQJ106 ♥853　　♦8　　♣AQJ8　　15 points
Answer: Double. You are too strong to overcall the spade suit. You will rebid 2♠ after partner's response of any suit to show a strong opening hand of 15+points.

#5 ♠QJ76　　♥4　　♦A987　　♣KJ54　　11 points
 Answer: Double, planning to support any suit bid by partner.

CHAPTER EIGHT
THE BOTTOM LINE

The Balancing Seat:

- You are in the <u>balancing seat</u> when your LHO opens one of a suit followed by two passes. Your pass would end the auction. Balancing is defined as a re-opening bid when the opponents' auction stops at a low level.

**Balance with a good suit, bid notrump or double.
Use the higher range of your
balancing point count requirements when vulnerable.**

 **<u>A Good Rule of Thumb is to Add Three Points to Your Hand
When You Make a Balancing Bid.</u>**

Best time to balance:

- Partner may have been forced to pass when holding decent values but with length in opponent's suit.

- You are short in the opponent's suit or you have a good five+card suit.

- If you pass, the opponents may make their bid at the one-level.

- You and your partner probably have half of the high card values available.

- If you defend, your bid will help your partner's choice of opening leads.

- You may also have a part score when the opponents have a part score.

- You may push the opponents to a higher level of bidding, and turn their plus into a minus.

#1

North
♠1095
♥103
♦8753
♣10732

West
♠KJ87
♥985
♦KQ92
♣A5

East
♠Q432
♥KQ4
♦A106
♣QJ9

South (Dealer)
♠A6
♥AJ762
♦J4
♣K864

South is the dealer with _____points and bids____; West passes; North passes; East bids____;
South passes; West bids____; North passes; East bids____; South passes; West bids____;
All Pass. What is the contract____? Who is the declarer____? Who leads the first card____?
What is the lead____?

#2

North
♠J872
♥74
♦Q7642
♣J7

West
♠953
♥AQ1083
♦1098
♣AQ

East
♠KQ106
♥5
♦KJ53
♣9852

South (Dealer)
♠A4
♥KJ962
♦A
♣K10643

South is the dealer with _____points and bids____; West passes; North passes; East makes a
takeout double; All Pass. What is the contract____? Who is the declarer____? Who leads the
first card____? What is the lead____?

#3

North
♠K83
♥106543
♦9
♣8643

West
♠954
♥QJ92
♦J1073
♣K5

East
♠AQJ1062
♥8
♦AKQ2
♣92

South (Dealer)
♠7
♥AK7
♦8654
♣AQJ107

South is the dealer with _____points and bids____; West passes; North passes; East with ____points; bids____; South passes; West bids____; North passes; East bids____; South passes; West bids____; All Pass. What is the contract____? Who is the declarer____? Who leads the first card____? What is the lead____?

#4

North
♠J87
♥65
♦QJ86
♣Q764

West
♠KQ3
♥843
♦1052
♣A832

East
♠10652
♥AQ10
♦K93
♣KJ10

South (Dealer)
♠A94
♥KJ972
♦A74
♣95

South is the dealer with _____points and bids____; West passes; North passes; East bids____; All Pass. What is the contract____? Who is the declarer____? Who leads the first card____? What is the lead____?

#5

North
♠KJ83
♥2
♦65432
♣432

West
♠Q105
♥Q64
♦AJ107
♣J105

East
♠76
♥J873
♦Q9
♣KQ987

South (Dealer)
♠A942
♥AK1095
♦K8
♣A6

South is the dealer with _____points and bids_____; All Pass.
What is the contract_____? Who is the declarer_____? Who leads the first card_____?
What is the lead_____?

#6

North
♠54
♥J6543
♦KJ876
♣5

West
♠K873
♥Q109
♦A43
♣KJ4

East
♠62
♥K8
♦1052
♣AQ10986

South (Dealer)
♠AQJ109
♥A72
♦Q9
♣732

South is the dealer with _____points and bids_____; West passes; North passes; East with
_____points bids_____; South passes; West bids_____; North passes; East bids_____; All Pass.
What is the contract_____? Who is the declarer_____? Who leads the first card_____?
What is the lead_____?

Answers to practice hands from page 111 - 112.

#1

South is the dealer with 14 points and bids 1♥; West passes; North passes; East with 14 points bids 1NT (balancing (12-14 points); South passes; West with 13 points bids 2♣ (Stayman); North passes; East bids 2♠; South passes; West bids 4♠; All Pass.
 East is the declarer in 4♠. South leads the ♣4.

#2

South is the dealer with 17 points and bids 1♥; West will **trap pass**; North passes;
East makes a takeout double; All Pass. South is the declarer in 1♥ X
West leads the ♦10.

By passing East's double, West shows heart length and points. If this was not the case, partner would have bid at his previous turn to speak.

#3

South is the dealer with 15 points and bids 1♣; West passes; North passes; East with 21 points (adding three points in the balancing seat) makes a takeout double; South passes; West bids 1♥; North passes; East jumps to 2♠; South passes; West bids 4♠; All Pass.
East is the declarer at 4♠. South leads the ♥A.

East doubles and jumps in spades to show a very strong hand. Even a 1♠ bid after doubling would show a 17-18 point count.

#4

South is the dealer with 13 points and bids 1♥; West passes; North passes;
East bids 1NT (12-14 balancing NT); All Pass.
East is the declarer in 1NT. South leads the ♥7.

#5

South is the dealer with 19 points bids 1♥; All Pass.
South is the declarer in 1♥. West leads the ♣J.

You have a good club suit and some defensive values in opponent's suit. Your hand is too weak to balance. Partner's passing indicates South may have a strong hand, and if you bid, the opponents may find a better trump fit.

#6

South is the dealer with 14 points and bids 1♠; West passes; North passes; East with 11 points bids 2♣; South passes; West bids 2NT, natural and invitational. East corrects to 3♣; All Pass.
East is the declarer in 3♣. South leads the ♣2 with no better lead.

NOTES

CHAPTER NINE

NEGATIVE DOUBLES   PENALTY DOUBLES

In the past, responder was only able to make penalty doubles after partner opened the bidding. Now responder has a use for a double other than a penalty double, **the negative double.** Modern bidding uses the term **negative double** to describe a bid that is similar to a takeout double used by responder to show the unbid suits.

Why use a negative double? The negative double is a solution to many bidding problems such as:

- Your RHO overcalls a suit bid by partner, and the overcall prevented you from bidding a four-card suit on the on one-level.
- The negative double can show two-suited hands.

Example: Partner 1♦, RHO 2♣. You have four hearts and four spades and only 8 points. You need five cards in a major and at least 10+points to bid the major at the two-level. If RHO had not overcalled, you would have an easy bid of 1♥ (bidding the suits "up the line"). Since the minors have been bid, your **negative double shows both majors.**

Requirements for one-level bids after an overcall:

- You need four+cards in the suit and 6+points to bid a new suit at the one-level.

Requirements for two-level bids after an overcall:

- You need five+cards in the suit and 10+points to bid a new suit at the two-level.
- You may have five+cards in the suit but not 10+points; you may have 10+points but not five+cards in the suit. If so, make a negative double.

AT A GLANCE

> **Your partner opens the bidding and your RHO overcalls:**
>
> **You can bid a new suit at the one-level.**
> **Your bids at the two-level show 5+cards in the suit and 10+points.**
>
> **When you <u>do not</u> have both requirements to bid a new suit at the two-level, cannot raise your partner or bid one no-trump over a one-level overcall...**
>
> **MAKE A NEGATIVE DOUBLE.**

Example: North
                           ♥AKQ7
West   Double - (shows four hearts)   East
1♠ (overcall)   Pass
                           South (Dealer)
                           1♣

South opens the bidding 1♣ and West overcalls 1♠. The spade overcall prevented North from bidding the heart suit at the one-level. North uses the negative double to show his four-card heart suit. North would also use the negative double with a five+card heart suit, and less than 10 points, as a free 2♥ bid promises a five+card heart suit and at least 10+points.

Negative doubles after one-level overcalls of partner's opening suit:

Partner 1♣ RHO overcalls 1♦	You may bid 1♥ or 1♠ with four+cards in the suit. This one-level bid of a major promises at least four cards in the suit and 6+points.
Partner 1♣ RHO overcalls 1♦	Double suggests four cards in both majors. With 5-4 in the majors, bid the 5-card major.
Partner 1♥ RHO overcalls 1♠	Double suggests four+cards in both minors.
Partner 1♣ RHO overcalls 1♥	With a four-card spade suit make a negative double. A free bid of 1♠ shows five+spades and 6+points.
Partner 1♣ RHO overcalls 1♠	Make a negative double to show a four-card heart suit, or five+hearts and less than 10 points.

Negative doubles after two-level overcalls of partner's opening suit:

Partner 1♦ RHO overcalls 2♣	Double shows four cards in both majors.
Partner 1♥ RHO overcalls 2♣/2♦	Double shows a four-card spade suit, or five+spades and less than 10 points.
Partner 1♠ RHO overcalls 2♦/2♣	Double shows a four+card heart suit, or five+hearts and less than 10 points.

Negative doubles after weak jump overcalls (WJO) by your RHO of partner's opening suit.

Partner 1♥ RHO overcalls 2♠ - WJO - Double shows both minors.	
Partner 1♣ RHO overcalls 2♦ - WJO Double shows both majors.	
Partner 1♣ RHO overcalls 2♠ - WJO Double shows a four+heart suit.	

116

Penalty Doubles: Penalty doubles are an important aspect of competitive bridge, especially in duplicate pair games. You double when you believe you can defeat a part score, game or slam contract bid by the opponents. Not doubling opponent's non-vulnerable sacrifice in a part score contract may allow the opponents to go down a few tricks in safety, since you will receive a lower score than if you had bid and made your contract.

When the opponents sacrifice, you must double or bid. However, you must be able to identify when the opponents are sacrificing. You may make a penalty double anytime during the auction. However, penalty doubles are usually made from the two-level or higher.

Your penalty double is based on a number of factors, including a trump misfit with partner, and you do not have enough points for game. Your opponents are in a part score or game contract. Determine if your side holds at least half (20 or more) of the combined high card points disclosed by the bidding during the auction. If so, the following rules of 10 and 12 may apply.

The Rule of 10: <u>Winners</u> in the opponents' trump suit. Add your expected trump tricks in the opponents' trump suit to the number of tricks the opponents need to fulfill the contract. If the answer is 10 or more, make a penalty double.

- One-level doubles: Declarer needs 7 tricks. You have 3 trump winners; 7+3 = 10
- Two-level doubles: Declarer needs 8 tricks. You have 2 trump winners; 8+2 = 10
- Three-level doubles: Declarer needs 9 tricks. You have 1 trump winner: 9+1 = 10

The Rule of 12: <u>Length</u> in the opponents' trump suit. Add the length of your trump holding in the opponents' trump suit.

- One-level doubles: Declarer needs 7 tricks. You have 5 trump cards; 7+5 = 12
- Two-level doubles: Declarer needs 8 tricks. You have 4 trump cards; 8+4 = 12
- Three level doubles: Declarer needs 9 tricks. You have 3 trump cards; 9+3 = 12
- Four-level doubles: Declarer needs 10 tricks. You have two trump cards; 10+2 = 12

Making a penalty double based only on your high card points may not be a good penalty double.

- Distributional factors must be considered. If you and partner have bid and rebid a suit, the opponents will be short in your suit, and will trump your high cards.
- You do not generally double a slam bid. If the opponents go down in the slam you will probably have a good result in any case.
- Usually only double a slam for an unusual lead such as the Lightner double, which asks partner to lead dummy's first bid suit.

Doubles are an important part of playing bridge, and good players will double more often than most players. However, your partnership must understand the different meanings of all doubles. Penalty doubles should never be confused with takeout doubles, negative doubles, support doubles, or maximal doubles. Easier said than done…

CHAPTER NINE
THE BOTTOM LINE

Partner opens the bidding and responder's RHO overcalls.
Responder uses the negative double to accurately describe his hand.

Your partner opens the bidding and your RHO overcalls:

You can bid a new suit at the one-level.
Bids at the two-level show 5+cards in the suit and 10+points.

When you <u>do not</u> have both requirements to bid a new suit at the two-level, cannot raise your partner or bid one no-trump …

MAKE A NEGATIVE DOUBLE.

Negative doubles after a one-level overcall of partner's opening suit:

Opener:	Responder's RHO overcalls
Opener bids 1♣ RHO overcalls 1♦	Bid 1♥ or 1♠ with a four+card suit. Double shows 4-4 cards in both majors.
Opener bids 1♥ RHO overcalls 1♠	Double shows 4-4 or more cards in both minors.
Opener bids 1♣ RHO overcalls 1♥	With a four-card spade suit, make a negative double. A bid of 1♠ shows five+spades and 6+points.
Opener bids 1♣ RHO overcalls 1♠	Make a negative double to show a four+heart suit, or a five+card heart suit and fewer than 10 points.

Negative doubles after a two-level overcall of partner's opening suit:

Opener:	Responder's RHO overcalls:
Opener 1♦ RHO overcalls 2♣	Double shows both 4-4 or more cards in both majors.
Opener bids 1♥ RHO overcalls 2♣/2♦	Double shows a four-card spade suit, or five+spades and fewer than 10 points.
Opener bids 1♠ RHO overcalls 2♦/2♣	Double shows a four-card heart suit, or five+card heart suit and fewer than 10 points

118

Negative double practice hands: **Answers on page 123 - 124.**

#1   North
                                      ♠QJ83
                                      ♥AKQ7
                                      ♦742
                                      ♣95

West   East
♠765   ♠42
♥85   ♥109643
♦AKJ63   ♦Q105
♣Q73   ♣A62

                                      South (Dealer)
                                      ♠AK109
                                      ♥J2
                                      ♦98
                                      ♣KJ1084

South is the dealer with _____points and bids___; East overcalls____; North makes a negative double; showing____; East bids____; South bids____; West passes: North bids____; All Pass. What is the contract____? Who is the declarer____? Who leads the first card____? What is the lead____?

#2   North (Dealer)
                                      ♠6
                                      ♥10765
                                      ♦QJ1098
                                      ♣AKQ

West   East
♠942   ♠KQJ873
♥9432   ♥Q
♦K76   ♦A4
♣974   ♣8632

                                      South
                                      ♠A105
                                      ♥AKJ8
                                      ♦532
                                      ♣J105

North is the dealer with _____points and bids ____; East overcalls ____; South makes a negative double showing____; West passes; North bids____; East passes; South bids____; All Pass. What is the contract____? Who is the declarer____? Who leads the first card____? What is the lead____?

119

#3

North
♠105
♥AJ109
♦962
♣K532

West
♠KQJ32
♥54
♦Q5
♣Q764

East
♠A74
♥632
♦KJ43
♣J109

South (Dealer)
♠986
♥KQ87
♦A1087
♣A8

South is the dealer with _____points and bids_____; West overcalls_____; North makes
a negative double showing_____; East bids_____; South bids_____; All Pass.
What is the contract_____? Who is the declarer_____? Who leads the first card_____?
What is the lead_____?

#4

North
♠9
♥84
♦AQ872
♣KQ1098

West
♠KQ1086
♥J63
♦K65
♣54

East
♠A732
♥1072
♦J1043
♣62

South (Dealer)
♠J54
♥AKQ95
♦9
♣AJ73

South is the dealer with _____points and bids _____; West overcalls_____; North makes a
negative double showing_____; East bids_____; South bids_____; West passes; North bids_____;
East passes; South bids_____; West passes; North bids_____; All Pass.
What is the contract_____? Who is the declarer_____? Who leads the first card_____?
What is the lead_____?

#5

North (Dealer)
♠32
♥K753
♦K4
♣AKJ54

West
♠Q94
♥84
♦98732
♣632

East
♠AJ1087
♥QJ2
♦QJ10
♣Q8

South
♠K65
♥A1096
♦A65
♣1097

North is the dealer with _____points and bids _____; East overcalls_____; South makes a negative double showing_____; West passes; North bids_____; East passes; South bids_____; All Pass. What is the contract_____? Who is the declarer_____? Who leads the first card_____? What is the lead_____?

#6

North
♠53
♥J63
♦AQJ87
♣Q42

West (Dealer)
♠K976
♥A108
♦32
♣AK98

East
♠QJ84
♥KQ75
♦109
♣1063

South
♠A102
♥942
♦K654
♣J75

West is the dealer with _____points and bids _____; North overcalls_____; East makes a negative double showing_____; South bids_____; West bids_____; All Pass.
What is the contract_____? Who is the declarer_____? Who leads the first card_____?
What is the lead_____?

#7

North
♠QJ75
♥AKJ4
♦854
♣54

West
♠863
♥103
♦KQ1092
♣Q86

East
♠42
♥98652
♦AJ3
♣1073

South (Dealer)
♠AK109
♥Q7
♦76
♣AKJ92

South is the dealer with _____points and bids ____; West overcalls____; North makes a negative double showing____; East bids____; South bids____; West passes; North bids____; All Pass. What is the contract____? Who is the declarer____? Who leads the first card____? What is the lead____?

#8

North
♠963
♥632
♦A853
♣654

West
♠10
♥10754
♦QJ76
♣KJ87

East (Dealer)
♠J842
♥AKJ8
♦10
♣AQ109

South
♠AKQ75
♥Q9
♦K942
♣32

East is the dealer with _____points and bids ____; South overcalls____; West makes a negative double showing____; North passes; East bids____; South passes; West bids____; All Pass. What is the contract____? Who is the declarer____? Who leads the first card____? What is the lead____?

Answers to practice hands on pages 121 - 122.

#1

South is the dealer with 13 points and bids 1♣; West overcalls 1♦; North with 12 points makes a negative double showing both majors; East bids 2♦; South bids 2♠; West passes: North now with 13 points (one point for the doubleton club) bids 4♠; All Pass.
South is the declarer in 4♠. West leads the ♦A.

- Declarer will need to guess clubs to make his game.

#2

North is the dealer with 13 points and bids 1♦; East overalls 1♠; South makes a negative double showing four hearts; South has 13 points, however he can't bid 2♥ as the bid would show a 5+card heart suit; West passes; North bids 2♥; East passes; South bids 4♥; All Pass.
North is the declarer in 4♥. East leads the ♠K.

- Declarer wins, cashes one top heart, and then plays on diamonds to hold his losers to three tricks in the red suits.

#3

South is the dealer with 13 points and bids 1♦; West overcalls 1♠; North with 8 points makes a negative double showing four hearts; East bids 2♠; South bids 3♥; All Pass.
South is the declarer in 3♥. West leads the ♠K.

- Declarer makes his contract by ruffing two clubs in his hand before drawing all the trumps.

#4

South is the dealer with 16 points and bids 1♥; West overcalls 1♠; North with 13 points makes a negative double showing both minors; East bids 2♠; South now with 18 points (two points for the singleton diamond) jumps to 4♣; West passes; North now with 16 points (two points for the singleton spade and one point for the doubleton heart) bids 4NT (Blackwood); East passes; South bids 5♥ (two aces); West passes; North bids 6♣; All Pass.
South is the declarer in 6♣. West leads the ♠K.

#5

North is the dealer with 15 points and bids 1♣; West overcalls 1♠; South makes a negative double showing four hearts; West passes; North bids 3♥; East passes; South bids 4♥; All Pass. North is the declarer in 4♥. East leads the ♦Q.

#6

West is the dealer with 14 points and bids 1♣; North overcalls 1♦; East makes a negative double showing both majors; South bids 2♦; West bids 2♠; All Pass. West is the declarer in 2♠. North leads the ♦A.

#7

South is the dealer with 18 points and bids 1♣; West overcalls 1♦; North makes a negative doubles showing both majors; East passes; South jumps to 3♠; West passes; North bids 4♠. All Pass.
South is the declarer in 4♠. West leads ♦K.

#8

East is the dealer with 15 points and bids 1♣; South overcalls 1♠; West makes a negative double showing at least four hearts; North passes; East now with 17 points bids 3♥; South passes; West now with 9 points (two points for the singleton spade) bids 4♥; All Pass.
East is the declarer in 4♥. South leads the ♠A.

CHAPTER TEN

THE REVERSE

Reverse bidding is an important bidding tool to show opener's point count and distribution. Reverses are part of standard bidding, and not a convention.

Basic bidding:

Basic bidding requires <u>responder</u> to respond with the lower ranking suits first by bidding the suits up-the-line (4-4 suits).

Example: Opener bids 1♣ - Responder bids 1♥ (responder may have both 4-card majors). By responder bidding his cheapest major, the bidding stays low and allows opener to rebid 1♠ with a 4-card spade suit.

- Your bids are usually made in the cheapest of your 4-card suits. Opener can then frequently rebid another suit on the one-level, keeping the bidding at a low level.
- If responder bids 1♠ initially, his bid usually denies a 4-card heart suit.

Basic bidding requires <u>opener</u> to bid his suits down-the-line. Opener with 5-5 or 5-4 in two suits will bid the higher-ranking suit first.

Example: Opener with 5-5 or 5-4 in the major suits will bid the spade suit first.

- By bidding spades first, opener can rebid hearts, allowing responder to take a preference to opener's first bid suit at the two-level.

Reverse Bids: Therefore, when opener bids a lower ranking suit at the one-level, and then rebids a higher-ranking suit at the two-level, this bid is called a "reverse" bid. The reverse forces responder to take a preference for opener's first bid suit at the three-level. Opener's needs at least 16+points to reverse the bidding sequence.

Opener can also show distributional two-suited hands by making a reverse.

- A reverse bid shows 5-4, 6-4, 6-5, 7-6 in two suits.
- The first suit bid must be <u>longer</u> than the rebid suit.
- The second suit bid must be <u>higher in rank</u> than the first suit bid.
- Partner must have bypassed your second suit with his response.
- Do not reverse with 5-5 in two suits. Holding 5-5 in two suits, bid the suits down the line, and bid your second suit twice if the opportunity arises to show five-cards in the second suit. You can jump shift in your second suit to show an 18+point count.

The reverse bid shows an opening hand with 16+points.
Opener's first bid suit must be longer than the reverse suit.
A reverse shows 5-4, 6-4, 6-5, 7-6 suit distribution.

Responder must give preference to partner's first bid suit at a higher level.

Example:

West	East
1♥	1♠
2♣ (not a reverse)	

East can easily support West's first bid suit at the two-level.

Example:

West	East
1♣	1♠
2♥ (a reverse)	

East must support West's first bid suit at the three-level.

Sample reverse hand:

West (Dealer)	1♦	1♠	East
♠65	2♥ (reverse)	4♥	♠K10843
♥AK102			♥Q986
♦KQ1092			♦10
♣A2			♣K109

- West with 17 points opens 1♦.
- East with 9 points bids 1♠. East will bid his 5-card spade suit first.
- West's 2♥ bid is a reverse bid, forcing responder to take preference for his first bid diamond suit at the three-level.
- East has four hearts, and partner's reverse bid promises at least four hearts and 16+points. East bids 4♥. This is a weaker call than 3♥.

West's reverse bid of 2♥ shows 16+points and four+card heart suit.
The reverse bid encouraged East to bid the 4♥ game.

Reverses are in play in competition.

Example:

West (Dealer)	North	East	South
1♣	Pass	1♠	2♦
2♥			

West's 2♥ rebid is still a reverse, as the 2♥ bid forces East to support West's first bid club suit at the three-level.

Responses after a reverse bid:

- **5-7 points: Bid 2NT or fourth suit if cheaper**. This is the weakest bid by responder and a **SIGN-OFF** asking opener to rebid **his first bid suit** with a minimum reverse.

- **5-7 points:** Bid 2NT first to show a weak hand, and then support opener's **second suit** to protect partner with a 19-21 point hand.

- **8+points:** Bid a forcing raise of opener's first bid suit with three+card support. Tends to deny support for opener's second suit.

- Responder's rebid of his own suit at the two-level suggests five or more cards, and while forcing for one round, does not guarantee game-forcing values. A jump in his own suit shows 12+points and a good suit.

- **8-11 points**: Bid 3NT with stoppers in the unbid suits.

- **8+points:** Bid a forcing raise of opener's second suit with four+card support.

- **12+points**: Jump in opener's first or second suit with 4+cards in the suit. Slam invitational, unless a jump to game.

Opener's rebid:

- Rebid first suit after a 2NT response with nothing extra, unless a more descriptive call is available.

- **19-21 points:** Rebid 3NT, or jump in the longer suit with game values after responder's 2NT relay, or bid the fourth suit yourself.

Opener's rebid to responder's fourth suit weak response.

- **17-18 points:** Rebid 2NT with a stopper in the fourth suit, a sign-off to responder.

- **19-21 points:** Rebid 3NT with stopper in the fourth suit. Opener can cue bid an overcall by his RHO to show maximum reverse.

One level bidding never constitutes a reverse:

Example: Opener   Responder

     1♣   1♥

     1♠ (not a reverse)

Reverses are on in competition:

Example: North (Dealer)	East	South	West
1♣	Pass	1♠	2♦
2♥ (a reverse)			

#1   North
                                          ♠ AK765
                                          ♥ 10932
                                          ♦ 863
                                          ♣ 10

West   East
♠ 843   ♠ QJ9
♥ Q4   ♥ K65
♦ QJ92   ♦ A1054
♣ 7542   ♣ J86

                                          South (Dealer)
                                          ♠ 102
                                          ♥ AJ87
                                          ♦ K7
                                          ♣ AKQ93

South is the dealer with____ points and bids____; West passes; North with ____points
bids____; East passes; South bids____; West passes; North bids____; All Pass.
What is the contract____? Who is the declarer____? Who leads the first card____?
What is the lead____?

#2   North
                                          ♠ KJ43
                                          ♥ 983
                                          ♦ Q98
                                          ♣ 1063

West   East
♠ Q652   ♠ A1098
♥ KJ4   ♥ Q752
♦ J32   ♦ 654
♣ J75   ♣ K2

                                          South (Dealer)
                                          ♠ 7
                                          ♥ A106
                                          ♦ AK107
                                          ♣ AQ984

South is the dealer with ____points and bids____; West passes; North with ____points
bids____; East passes; South bids____; West passes; North bids____; East passes; South
bids____; All Pass. What is the contract____? Who is the declarer____? Who leads the first
card____? What is the lead____?

#3

North
♠QJ87
♥Q8
♦J765
♣K76

West
♠A9653
♥542
♦Q10
♣1095

East
♠42
♥A763
♦43
♣QJ832

South (Dealer)
♠K10
♥KJ109
♦AK982
♣A4

South is the dealer with _____points and bids____; West passes; North bids____; East passes; South bids____; North bids____; East passes; South bids____; All Pass.
What is the contract____? Who is the declarer____? Who leads the first card____?
What is the lead____?

#4

North
♠K1064
♥AQ
♦A7
♣J10762

West
♠Q532
♥J952
♦J832
♣5

East
♠AJ87
♥108763
♦654
♣3

South (Dealer)
♠9
♥K4
♦KQ109
♣AKQ984

South is the dealer with _____points and bids____; West passes; North bids____; East passes; South bids____; West passes; North bids____; East passes; South bids____; West passes; North bids____; East passes; South bids____; All Pass.
What is the contract____? Who is the declarer____? Who leads the first card____?
What is the lead____?

#5

North
♠Q9643
♥1098
♦Q107
♣Q4

West
♠K102
♥A43
♦654
♣J762

East
♠AJ5
♥J52
♦32
♣A9853

South (Dealer)
♠87
♥KQ76
♦AKJ98
♣K10

South is the dealer with _____points and bids____; West passes; North with ____points bids____; East passes; South bids____; West passes; North bids____; East passes; South bids____; All Pass. What is the contract____? Who is the declarer____? Who leads the first card____? What is the lead____?

#6

North
♠KQ954
♥K73
♦Q108
♣K6

West
♠J72
♥852
♦A764
♣J75

East (Dealer)
♠A
♥AJ109
♦K5
♣AQ10982

South
♠10863
♥Q64
♦J932
♣43

East is the dealer with _____points and bids____; South passes; West with ____points bids____; North overcalls____; East bids____; South passes; West bids____; North passes; East bids____; West bids____; North passes; East bids____: All Pass.
What is the contract____? Who is the declarer____? Who leads the first card____?
What is the lead____?

#7

North
♠AQ64
♥AQJ5
♦Q653
♣6

West
♠J1093
♥8764
♦72
♣Q109

East
♠K87
♥K1092
♦984
♣873

South (Dealer)
♠52
♥3
♦AKJ10
♣AKJ542

South is the dealer with _____points and bids____; West passes; North with ____points bids____; East passes; South bids____; West passes; North bids____; East passes; South bids ____; West passes; North bids____; East passes; South bids____; All Pass.
What is the contract____? Who is the declarer____? Who leads the first card____?
What is the lead____?

#8

North
♠J954
♥1054
♦Q74
♣954

West (Dealer)
♠A8
♥2
♦A832
♣AKQ1073

East
♠1032
♥QJ96
♦KJ65
♣J6

South
♠KQ76
♥AK873
♦109
♣82

West is the dealer with____ points and bids____; North passes; East with ____points bids____; South passes; West bids____; North passes; East bids____; South passes; West bids____; All Pass. What is the contract____? Who is the declarer____? Who leads the first card____? What is the lead____?

Answers to practice hands on 128 - 131

#1

South the dealer with 18 points and bids 1♣; West passes; North with 8 points bids 1♠; East passes; South bids 2♥ (reverse); West passes; North bids 4♥; All Pass. South is the declarer in 4♥. West leads the ♦Q.

- Declarer wins the second diamond and uses a spade entry to run the ♥10, then ruffs a diamond, ruffs a club to dummy, and repeats the heart finesse for the contract.

#2

South is the dealer with 17 points and bids 1♣; West passes; North with 7 points bids 1♠; East passes; South bids 2♦ (reverse); West passes; North bids a **2NT weak sign off** (asks partner to return to first bid club suit;) East passes; South bids 3♣; All Pass. South is the declarer in 3♣. West leads the ♥4.

#3

South is the dealer with 19 points and bids 1♦; West passes; North with 9 points bids 1♠; East passes; South bids 2♥ (reverse); West passes; North bids 3♦; East passes; South bids 3NT; All Pass. South is the declarer in 3NT. West leads the ♠5.

#4

South is the dealer with 19 points and bids 1♣; West passes; North with 15 points bids 1♠; East passes; South bids 2♦ (reverse); West passes; North jumps to 4♣ with real extras and good support; East passes; South bids 4NT (Blackwood); West passes; North bids 5♥ (two aces); East passes; South bids 6♣; All Pass. South is the declarer in 6♣. West leads the ♥2, the unbid suit.

#5

South is the dealer with 17 points and bids 1♦; West passes; North with 7 points bids 1♠; East passes; South bids 2♥ (reverse); West passes; North bids 2NT (weak); East passes; South bids 3♦; All Pass. South is the declarer in 3♦. West leads the ♣2.

- East takes the ♣A and returns the suit. Declarer should play on spades to set up the suit and avoid having to guess in hearts.

#6

East is the dealer with 20 points and bids 1♣; South passes; West with 6 points bids 1♦; North overcalls 1♠; East bids 2♥ (reverse); South passes; West bids 2NT; North passes; East now with 22 points (two points for the singleton spade) bids 3♠, **a forcing cue bid to show better than a minimum reverse;** South passes; West bids 4♣; North passes; East bids 5♣; All Pass. East is the declarer in 5♣. South leads the ♠3.

After a spade lead, declarer wins in hand, and leads a diamond to dummy to run the ♣J planning to drop the eight from hand if North plays low to save an entry to dummy. When North covers the ♣J, declarer wins, draws trump, and then plays on hearts for 11 tricks.

#7

South is the dealer with 18 points and bids 1♣; West passes; North with 15 points bids 1♥; East passes; South bids 2♦; West passes; North jumps to 4♦ showing 12+points; East passes; South now with 21 points (two points for the singleton heart and one point for the doubleton spade) bids 4NT (Blackwood); West passes; North bids 5♥ (two aces); East passes; South bids 6♦. All pass. South is the declarer in 6♦. West leads the ♠J.

- Declarer wins the ♠A in dummy, plays the ♣AK from his hand, and crossruffs hearts and clubs for 12 tricks, making each trump separately.

#8

West is the dealer with 19 points and bids 1♣; North passes; East with 8 points bids 1♥; South passes; West bids 2♦ (reverse); North passes; East with 8+points bids 3♦; South passes; West bids 3NT; All Pass. West is the declarer in 3NT. North leads the ♠4.

NOTES

CHAPTER ELEVEN

DECLARER PLAY   DEFENSE

Declarer play:

Declarer should try to ruff on the "short side" or dummy side of the trump suit. Ruffing on the short side can produce extra trump tricks.

- Dummy counts his **void** points equal to dummy's number of trumps.

Example: If the trump suit is spades:

Dummy: ♠ J1043, ♥---, ♦A7652, ♣Q986 - 7 HCP+ one point for 5th diamond = 8 points. Dummy's four spades allows four points with the heart void. Dummy points = 12 points.

Declarer's trump suit:

- Declarer should only count three points for a void after a hearing a fit in a suit with partner.

    Why? Declarer's trumps will usually produce the number of tricks equal to the number of trumps declarer's hand. Declarer's trumps usually do not produce extra tricks.

Example: AKQ1098 in declarer's hand will usually only provide only six trump tricks. Ruffing in the "long hand" may not produce extra trump tricks.

Ruffing on the long side:

- However, there may be hands where declarer may win more trump tricks by using the trumps in declarer's hand.

- In the hand below, you are left in a contract with few trumps in dummy and a weak trump suit in declarer's hand.

- Rather than pull trump, you trump tricks in the declarer's hand to make extra tricks.

Example: 2♠ contract: Dummy: ♠ ---   ♥A965   ♦A10754   ♣A1065
                Declarer: ♠QJ10863 ♥K83   ♦632   ♣3

- Declarer has four tricks outside of the trump suit. Declarer can make three extra trump tricks by trumping in his own hand. Four quick tricks plus three trump tricks and one trick from the ♠QJ10 = 8 tricks.

135

The Crossruff:

- The purpose of the crossruff is to make extra trump tricks by ruffing suits in the dummy and in the declarer's hand.
- **One of the most important aspects of the crossruff is to first cash winning tricks in the side suits early in the play.** As you are crossruffing, the defenders may be discarding their losers in the side suits. When you finally play your winners, defendants may be able trump your winning tricks.
- You also may lose control of the trump suit by crossruffing, and there is a danger of defendants over-ruffing in a later stage of the crossruff play. At that time, you need to ruff with high trumps to prevent a defendant from over-ruffing and leading a trump. Good defendants may lead trumps to prevent further crossruffs.

The Ruffing Finesse:

- Declarer uses a ruffing finesse with a broken high card sequence in one hand and a singleton or void in the same suit in the other hand.

Example: Dummy
   ♠AQJ109

   Declarer
   ♠3

- Declarer leads the ♠3 to the ♠A in dummy.
- The ♠Q is led from dummy. If East covers with the ♠K, South ruffs the ♠K setting up the good ♠J109 in dummy.
- However, if the ♠Q is not covered with the ♠K, South discards a loser from his hand. A loser on loser play. If West takes the ♠K, the ♠J109 are now good tricks in dummy.

Another type of ruffing finesse is the example in the hand below.

Example:

Contract: 6♥	North	Dummy:	♠Q	♥KJ942	♦K987	♣1076
Lead: ♠3	South	Declarer:	♠J1092	♥AQ10876	♦---	♣AQ2

- West leads the ♠3 won by East ♠A. East did not play the ♠K, lower of touching honors. **Declarer places the ♠K in the West hand.**
- East shifts to the ♣3. **South should not take the club finesse.**
- South wins the ♣A, draws trump, and leads the ♠J for a **ruffing finesse of West's ♠K.**
- If West covers the ♠J with the ♠K, South will trump in dummy and come back to his hand with a diamond ruff to discard losing clubs in dummy on the good ♠109 in his hand.
- If West does not cover the ♠J, South discards a club from dummy. He returns to his hand with a trump and leads the ♠10 to repeat the ruffing finesse in the spade suit.

Crossruff practice hand:

#1   North
                                  ♠KQ102
                                  ♥875
                                  ♦A10643
                                  ♣3

West   East
♠54   ♠763
♥A103   ♥<u>K</u>Q64
♦QJ852   ♦K9
♣J54   ♣K1096

                                  South (Dealer)
                                  ♠AJ98
                                  ♥J92
                                  ♦7
                                  ♣AQ872

Contract is 4♠   East leads ♥K
Bidding: East and West pass throughout the bidding.

South (Dealer)	North
1♣	1♠
2♠	3♦ (help suit try)
4♠	All Pass

- East-West take the first three heart tricks ending in the West hand.
- West leads the ♦Q.
- North wins the ♦A, cashes the ♣A, and cross ruffs diamonds and clubs.
- North-South trumps are high and there is no danger of over-ruffing by the opponents.
- Declarer cross ruffs diamonds and clubs making eight trump tricks, plus the ♣A+♦A = 10 tricks. 4♠ contract made.

Had defenders shifted to trumps, declarer would have needed to take the club finesse for the tenth trick.

Crossruff practice hand:

#2
                        North (Dealer)
                        ♠3
                        ♥Q1097
                        ♦AQ975
                        ♣AK5

West
♠<u>K</u>Q1074
♥5
♦43
♣96432

East
♠985
♥642
♦KJ1082
♣Q10

                        South
                        ♠AJ62
                        ♥AKJ83
                        ♦6
                        ♣J87

Contract is 6♥   **West leads ♠K**
Bidding: East and West pass throughout the bidding.

North (Dealer)	South
1♦	1♥
3♥	3♠ (control)
4♣ (control)	4♦ (control)
4NT (Blackwood)	5♥ (two aces)
6♥	All Pass

- South counts four winners in side suits.
- South knows he must make eight tricks in the trump suit by crossruffing each trump independently to make the 6♥ contract.

South must cash the ♣AK early in the crossruff to prevent East from sluffing clubs and trumping declarer's club winners.

Crossruff practice hand:

#3

North
♠ Q842
♥ 3
♦ AQJ5
♣ 9832

West
♠ 1075
♥ K1095
♦ 83
♣ QJ105

East
♠ KJ963
♥ Q62
♦ 762
♣ 74

South (Dealer)
♠ A
♥ AJ874
♦ K1094
♣ AK6

Contract is 6♦   West leads ♣Q
Bidding: East and West pass throughout the bidding.

South (Dealer)	North
1♥	1♠
3♦ (jump shift)	4♦
4NT	5♦ (one ace)
6♦	All Pass

- West leads the ♣Q and declarer plays the ♣A.
- South must play the ♣K before starting the crossruff.
- South has a club loser and must ruff heart losers.
- South plans to ruff the major suits. The best line is ♣A, ♥A, heart ruff and a club towards the king in case clubs are 5-1.
- Then ♠A, heart ruff and continue the crossruff.

South has eight trump tricks, two club tricks and the ♥A and ♠A for 12 tricks.

#4 Ruffing Finesse:

North (Dealer)
♠ A954
♥ 106
♦ AQJ109
♣ J8

West
♠ 8
♥ **K**QJ92
♦ 752
♣ K432

East
♠ J7
♥ 8753
♦ K864
♣ 765

South
♠ KQ10632
♥ A4
♦ 3
♣ AQ109

Contract is 6♠   West leads ♥K
Bidding: East and West pass throughout the bidding.

North (Dealer)	South
1♦	1♠
2♠	4NT (Blackwood)
5♥ (2 aces)	6♠
All Pass	

- West leads the ♥K and declarer has a heart loser and possible club loser if the finesse of the ♣K fails. Declarer pulls two rounds of trumps with the ♠KQ.
- Declarer will lead the ♦3 to the ♦A in dummy and lead the ♦Q for a ruffing finesse.
- If RHO covers with the ♦K, declarer will trump and sluff three club losers on the good diamonds in dummy. There is no need to finesse for the ♣K.
- If RHO does not play the ♦K, declarer will sluff his heart loser on the ♦Q.
- This is a loser on loser play.

LHO may win the ♦K, however, declarer can later sluff the club losers on the good diamonds in dummy.

DEFENSE:

Suit preference signals:

- Partner leads the ♠A in declarer's 4♥ contract. Dummy has a singleton spade and will be void in the spade suit after the lead.

- **You want to signal partner to lead the diamond suit. Play a high spade for a suit preference signal.** Obviously, you do not want partner to play another spade with the void in dummy. Your high spade asks partner to lead the higher-ranking suit in dummy other than the heart trump suit. Diamonds are higher ranking than clubs.

- Your partner leads high-low in your suit showing a doubleton. You plan to play king then ace of the suit and provide partner with a ruff. **The card you lead back to partner for the ruff signals the suit you want partner to lead back to you to provide another ruff for partner.** A high card shows the higher-ranking suit in dummy, and a low card shows the lower ranking suit in dummy, other than the trump suit.

Attitude and count:

- You usually show **attitude,** when partner leads a suit. You can show you like the suit by playing a high card (or a low card by agreement if you play "upside down" attitude).

- If partner knows your attitude by seeing the outcome of the trick, then signal **count.** Standard count of a high-low play of the suit shows an even number of cards, and a low-high play of the suit shows an odd number of cards.

Play lower of touching honors:

- Partner leads a low card in a suit followed by a low card in dummy. You have KQ in the suit. **Play the queen, lower of touching honors.** The same is true of any touching honors such as the 10 from J10, the J from QJ, etc. If you are going to retain the lead with e.g. a doubleton ace-king you can win the first trick with the ace, then play the king to make that clear.

Holding the ace of trump:

- When holding the ace of the opponents trump suit, you may want to wait to play the ace until the dummy is depleted of trumps before taking your ace of trumps. This decision is usually made when you think declarer will want to trump losers in dummy.

- It is certainly sensible to plan in advance when the right moment to take or duck your ace.

Keep equal length with the suits in dummy:

- When discarding, defenders should attempt to keep winners and throw losers. All things being equal, try to retain an equal number of cards (parity) with the length of suits in dummy, and discard from other suits if possible.

Cover an honor with an honor:

- Only cover an honor only when you hope to promote a lesser card in your hand or partner's hand.

- Do <u>not</u> cover when you can see the J10 or 10 in dummy. There is no reason to cover, as you will not promote the 10 in your hand or partner's hand.

- Do not cover the first of touching honors such as the QJ in dummy, and be wary of covering the queen from the closed hand with the ace in dummy. The closed hand likely has the jack as well. However, try to cover from a doubleton king.

Lead directing doubles:

- When your RHO makes an artificial bid such as Stayman, or Jacoby transfer bids, you expect partner to be on lead.

- Make a lead directing double holding a suit with four+cards and two+honors in the suit. These calls are not without risk, but you often help your partner find the best lead this way

Trump leads:

- A trump lead is usually the best lead against a sacrifice by the opponents.

- Make a "passive" lead against a grand slam or 6NT slam, and usually a more aggressive lead against other slams. However, it's usually **not** wise to lead low from a king against any slam contract, unless you can see that declarer may be about to establish a suit for discards.

Trump promotion:

- In most cases, giving declarer a ruff and sluff is not a good idea.

- However, there are times when giving a ruff and sluff will promote a trump trick in partner's hand.

- The ruff and sluff may not help declarer when there are good side-suits in the dummy, or declarer clearly has no losers outside trumps.

Trump promotion practice hand:

#1

North
- ♠742
- ♥J3
- ♦AQJ4
- ♣9762

West
- ♠A10
- ♥**A**KQ854
- ♦K85
- ♣83

East
- ♠J5
- ♥1062
- ♦9762
- ♣J1054

South (Dealer)
- ♠KQ9863
- ♥97
- ♦103
- ♣AKQ

Contract is 4♠ West leads ♥A
Bidding:

South (Dealer)	West	North	East
1♠	2♥	2♠	Pass
3♠	Pass	4♠	All Pass

- West leads the ♥A and East's play of the ♥2 shows odd number of hearts.
- As West you count two hearts in dummy, and the count shows declarer with two hearts. Your ♦K is finessable, and you know from the bidding that declarer must have two of the top three clubs. Your only hope of setting the contract is to continue with the ♥K followed by the ♥Q, though you are giving declarer a ruff and sluff. Declarer ruffs the third round of hearts. To pull trump, South must play a low spade to the ♠K in his hand and West takes the ♠A. Now West leads another heart hoping partner has the ♠J and can ruff the fourth round of the suit. East ruffs the fourth round of the heart suit with the ♠J.

To prevent an overruff, South must ruff with the ♠Q promoting West's ♠10 as the setting trick.

#2   Puzzler:

North (Dealer)
♠2
♥AK87
♦65
♣KQ10643

West (Dealer)
♠543
♥64<u>3</u>
♦KJ74
♣875

East
♠A6
♥QJ1092
♦A32
♣J92

South
♠KQJ10987
♥5
♦Q1098
♣A

Contract is 4♠   West leads ♥3
Bidding:

North (Dealer)	East	South	West
1♣	1♥	1♠	Pass
2♣	Pass	4♠	All Pass

- You have four losers, three diamonds and the ♠A
- How do you avoid three diamond losers?

 Answer.

Play the ♥A from dummy. Then play the ♥K and sluff the ♣A from declarer's hand on the ♥K in dummy. This unblocking play enables you to discard losing diamonds from declarer's hand on the club winners in dummy.

CHAPTER TWELVE

SCORING THE GAME

Duplicate or Chicago Style scoring are outlined in this chapter. Although based on rubber bridge, duplicate and Chicago scoring are more in use today than rubber bridge scoring.

 **GAME AND SLAM BONUS POINTS**

Non-Vulnerable Bonus Points.

Game	300 points
Small slam	500 points
Grand slam	1000 points

Vulnerable Bonus Points.

Game	500 points
Small slam	750 points
Grand slam	1500 points

Trick Points

> ♠Spades = 30 points per trick
>
> ♥Hearts = 30 points per trick
>
> ♦Diamonds = 20 points per trick
>
> ♣Clubs = 20 points per trick
>
> No Trump = 40 points for first trick, 30 points
> for each additional trick

The scoring below describes major suit games and slams. Adjust per trick scores for games and slams in the minor suits, notrump contracts and bonus points for slams.

Add Bonus Points Plus Per Trick Points:

Game points: Add game bonus points + per trick points to arrive a game scores.

Non-vulnerable game: 300 bonus points+4 tricks x 30 points = 120 points = 420 total points.
Vulnerable game: 500 bonus points+4 tricks x 30 points = 120 points = 620 total points.

Slam points: Game bonus points +slam bonus points + per trick points = slam scores.

Non-vulnerable small slam: 500 slam bonus points+300 game bonus points+ 6 trick
Total points = 980 for non-vulnerable small slam

Vulnerable small slam: 750 slam bonus points+500 game bonus points+6 tricks
Total points = 1430 for vulnerable small slam.

Part Score Points:

- Part scores are bids below games or slam contracts. When your partnership does not have the required points to bid game, you will "settle" for a part score.

- **Vulnerability is not a factor in making part scores.** You make the same 50 bonus + per trick points. You only make extra bonus points when you bid and make games or slams.

Example: You bid 3♠ and you make 4♠ or an "overtrick". You receive the 50 bonus points for the part score, and per trick points of 30 points per trick (4 x 30 = 120+50 bonus points) for a total score of 170 points. If you bid a 4♠ game, you would receive an additional 300 bonus points for a non-vulnerable game and have a score of 420 points.

You get <u>50 bonus points</u> plus per trick points for making part scores

---

Spade and heart part scores - 1, 2 or 3 ♠/♥

1♠/1♥ = 30 for 1 trick + 50 bonus part score = 80 points
2♠/2♥ = 60 for 2 tricks + 50 bonus part score = 110 points
3♠/3♥ = 90 for 3 tricks + 50 bonus part score = 140 points

Diamond and club part scores - 1, 2, 3, or 4 ♦/♣

1♦/1♣ = 20 for 1 trick + 50 part score = 70 points
2♦/2♣ = 40 for 2 tricks + 50 part score = 90 points
3♦/3♣ = 60 for 3 tricks + 50 part score = 110 points
4♦/4♣ = 80 for 4 tricks + 50 part score = 130 points

Notrump – 1NT or 2NT

1NT = 40 for first trick + 50 part score = 90 points
2NT = 70 for 2 tricks + 50 part score = 120 points

Vulnerability is a factor when you go down tricks.

- In a non-vulnerable contract, you lose 50 points for every trick you go down and in a vulnerable contract; you lose 100 points for every trick you "go down".

Penalties for going down in a doubled contract.
A defender may double your contract and if so:

- Non-vulnerable doubled: Down - 1 = 100; 2 = 300; 3 = 500; 4 = 800; 5 = 1100 etc.
- Vulnerable doubled: Down - 1 = 200; 2 = 500; 3 = 800; 4 = 1100 etc.

How many points did you earn for making these contracts?
Answers at bottom of page

V is for vulnerable   NV is for non-vulnerable

#1   3♠_____   2♠_____   1♠_____   V 4♠_____

#2   1♥_____   V 6♥_____   V 4♥_____   3♥_____

#3   V 5♦_____   3♦_____   2♦_____   NV 6♦_____

#4   V 3NT_____   2NT_____   1NT_____   V 5NT_____

#5   NV 6NT_____   V7 NT_____   V 7♠_____   NV 7♣_____

#6   NV 5♦_____   4♦_____   2♥_____   V 6♦_____

 __Answers: How many points did you win in the contracts?__

#1   3♠ - 140   2♠ - 110   1♠ - 80   V 4♠ - 620

#2   1♥ - 80   V 6♥ - 1430   V 4♥ - 620   3♥ - 140

#3   V 5♦ - 600   3♦ - 110   2♦ - 90   NV 6♦ - 920

#4   V 3NT - 600   2NT - 120   1NT - 90   V 5NT - 660

#5   NV 6NT - 990   V 7NT - 2220   V 7♠ - 2210   NV 7♣ - 1440

#6   NV 5♦ - 600   4♦ - 130   2♥ - 110   V 6♦ - 1370

How many points did you win or lose?   **Answers bottom of page**

<u>D - Doubled Contract</u>   <u>Vulnerable - V</u>   <u>Non-vulnerable - NV</u>

Contract: 4♠ <u>D</u> V – you only made 3: how many points to opponents_____?

Contract: 2♠ – you made 3: how many points to you_____?

Contract: 3NT V – you made 3: how many points to you_____?

Contract: 4 ♥ NV – you only made 2: how many points to opponents_____?

Contract: 5♦ NV – you made 4: how many points to opponents_____?

Contract: 2♣ – you made 2: how many points to you_____?

Contract: 4♥ V – you made 4: how many points to you_____?

Contract: 6♠ V – you made 6: how many points to you_____?

Contract: 4♠ V – you only made 3: how many points to opponents_____?

Contract: 2NT V – you made 3: how many points to you_____?

 Answers: How many points did you win or lose in the following contracts?

Contract: 4♠ <u>D</u> V – you only made 3: down one doubled - 200 points to opponents.

Contract: 2♠ – you made 3: 140 points to you.

Contract: 3NT V – you made 3: 600 points to you for vulnerable 3NT game.

Contract: 4♥ NV – you only made 2: down 2 NV - 100 points to opponents.

Contract: 5♦ NV – you made 4: down one NV - 50 points to opponents.

Contract: 2♣ – you made 2: 90 points to you.

Contract: 4♥ V – you made 4: 620 points to you for vulnerable 4♥ game.

Contract: 6♠ V – you made 6: 1430 points to you for vulnerable 6♠ small slam.

Contract: 4♠ V – you made 3, down one vulnerable – 100 points to opponents.

Contract: 2NT V – you made 3: 150 points to you for part score.

Do you bid a game or part score?   Answers for #3 - #9 on page 151 - 152

D= Doubleton; S = Singleton; V = Void; Resp = Responder; PT SC = Part Score
#1 and #2 are sample hands with answers.

OPENER	BID	BID	RESP	GAME	PT SC
♠KQ1098	1♠	2♠	♠543	4♠	
♥K52	3♠	4♠	♥QJ76		
♦AK6			♦43		
♣32			♣KQ54		
points = 16	17+1 D♣		points = 9 +1 D♦		

#2

OPENER	BID	BID	RESP	GAME	PT SC
♠A2	1♥	1NT	♠543	4♥	
♥KQ10432	3♥	4♥	♥A6		
♦Q76			♦K10432		
♣A6			♣Q54		
points = 17			points = 10		

#3

OPENER	BID	BID	RESP	GAME	PT SC
♠Q109			♠52		
♥AQ765			♥8432		
♦1098			♦QJ43		
♣A2			♣KQ5		
points =			points =		

#4

OPENER	BID	BID	RESP	GAME	PT SC
♠AQ98			♠1076		
♥Q1075			♥10432		
♦42			♦AK2		
♣AJ2			♣1098		
points =			points =		

#5

OPENER	BID	BID	RESP	GAME	PT SC
♠KQ1098			♠J42		
♥AKJ2			♥76		
♦32			♦AJ76		
♣A8			♣J432		
points =			points =		

#6

OPENER	BID	BID	RESP	GAME	PT SC
♠KJ1082			♠Q6		
♥KJ10			♥Q92		
♦A32			♦K765		
♣J10			♣Q743		
points =			points =		

#7

OPENER	BID	BID	RESP	GAME	PT SC
♠KJ10964			♠A2		
♥5			♥A9		
♦A65			♦K10982		
♣K65			♣J1098		
points =			points =		

#8

OPENER	BID	BID	RESP	GAME	PT SC
♠AJ1086			♠KQ32		
♥AJ6			♥KJ6		
♦83			♦J109		
♣KQ4			♣632		
points =			points =		

#9

OPENER	BID	BID	RESP	GAME	PT SC
♠10652			♠QJ43		
♥AJ9			♥KQ76		
♦KJ103			♦Q54		
♣AK			♣642		
points =			points =		

Do you bid game or part score (Part Sc)? Answers for quiz on pages 149 -150

#3

OPENER	BID	BID	RESP	GAME	PT SC
♠J109	1♥	2♥	♠52		2♥
♥AQ765	Pass		♥8432		
♦1098			♦QJ43		
♣A2			♣KQ5		
Points = 12			Points = 9		
			1 points D♠		

#4

OPENER	BID	BID	RESP	GAME	PT SC
♠AQ98	1♣	1♥	♠1076		2♥
♥Q1075	2♥	Pass	♥10432		
♦42			♦AK2		
♣AJ2			♣1098		
Points = 13			Points = 7		

#5

OPENER	BID	BID	RESP	GAME	PT SC
♠KQ1098	1♠	2♠	♠J42	4♠	
♥AKJ2	4♠	Pass	♥76		
♦32			♦AJ76		
♣A8			♣J432		
Points = 18	20 points		Points = 8	1 point	
	2 D♦ ♣			for D♥	

#6

OPENER	BID	BID	RESP	GAME	PT SC
♠KJ1082	1♠	1NT	♠Q6		1NT
♥KJ10	Pass		♥Q92		
♦A32			♦K765		
♣J10			♣Q743		
Points = 14			Points = 9		

#7

OPENER	BID	BID	RESP	GAME	PT SC
♠KJ10964	1♠	2♦	♠A2	4♠	
♥5	2♠	4♠	♥A9		
♦A65	Pass		♦K10982		
♣K65			♣J1098		
Points = 13	Six-card spade		Points = 13	14 points 1 D♥	

#8

OPENER	BID	BID	RESP	GAME	PT SC
♠AJ10	1NT	2♣ Stayman	♠KQ32	3NT	
♥AJ86	2♦	3NT	♥KJ5		
♦863	Pass		♦J109		
♣KQ4			♣632		
Points = 15			Points = 10		

#9

OPENER	BID	BID	RESP	GAME	PT SC
♠652	1NT	2♣ Stayman	♠QJ4	4♥	
♥AJ92	2♥	4♥	♥KQ76		
♦KJ103	Pass		♦Q54		
♣AK			♣642		
Points = 16			Points = 10		

AMERICAN CONTRACT BRIDGE LEAGUE

STYLES OF BRIDGE GAMES

American Contract Bridge League:

The American Contract Bridge League (ACBL) was founded in 1937, and celebrated its 75th birthday in 2012. ACBL is the largest bridge organization in the world with over 160,000 members in the United States, Canada, Mexico and Bermuda.

ACBL is a non-profit organization, dealing with the rules of bridge, education, and sanctioned clubs and tournament games. You can contact ACBL to find duplicate games in your area.

ACBL web site is www.acbl.org; toll free telephone number 800-467-1623.

Styles of Bridge: Duplicate, rubber and Chicago style bridge.

The scoring used in duplicate and Chicago bridge derived from rubber bridge scoring as did the terms **vulnerable contracts and non-vulnerable contracts.**

Rubber Bridge:

- In rubber bridge scoring, the first game on your score earns non-vulnerable bonus points.

- When you or your opponents have a "game on", the team becomes vulnerable. The team with no game is non-vulnerable.

- When you are vulnerable, you win more bonus points when you make games, and lose more points when your game or part score goes down tricks.

- If you win two games before the opponents can win two games, you win the "rubber" and added bonus points. In rubber bridge, extra points are also given for honor cards in trump suits.

- When a team has a part score (partial) in rubber bridge, they need only make other part scores to create the second game and win the rubber.

- This method of scoring left many hands bid only to partial games with game going points. Many hands were underbid, as only partials were needed to win the rubber.

- Today, duplicate and Chicago style bridge are more popular than rubber bridge as most players prefer to bid hands to the maximum level of their combined point count.

Chicago Bridge:

- Chicago style bridge is used in home games. Players draw for the high card to become the dealer. Duplicate style scoring is usually used in Chicago bridge.

- The deal proceeds clockwise around the table after each hand.

- No one is vulnerable on the first hand. The 2nd hand dealer and partner are vulnerable, 3rd hand dealer and partner are vulnerable, and 4th hand all players are vulnerable.

Duplicate Bridge:

- Duplicate bridge is played throughout the world. Virtually every locale has numerous duplicate bridge clubs, and there are hundreds of tournaments played yearly throughout the United States and internationally.

- In addition, computer online duplicate games can be played any time of the day or night. Bridgebase online is a popular site for on-line bridge. www.bridgebaseonline.com.

- Duplicate play is considered an equitable form of bridge, as winning does not merely rely on holding high cards. Good defense is equally important to win in the game.

Duplicate play:

- Duplicate bridge games are arranged as numbered tables where partnerships play in positions of either North/South or East/West.

- Cards are placed in "boards" (card holders) and, after the play of the cards in a round, the boards are passed to the next lowered numbered table.

- The Mitchell movement is one type of duplicate play. The boards are passed to lower tables and the E/W players move to higher tables after each round.

- The N/S players remain stationary at their opening tables. The boards and E/W players continue to move until all the boards are played in duplicate bridge session.

- A director runs the game, and inputs all the scores into an ACBL computer program which scores percentage points for each team.

- The N/S teams compete against other N/S teams, which also applies for the E/W teams. Teams with the highest scores win the duplicate session with others teams placing 2nd, 3rd, 4th etc. Duplicate bridge is usually played in duplicate clubs, and can also be played in home games with two or more tables in play.

GLOSSARY

Artificial bid: A bid that conveys a different meaning than the actual bid made.

Balanced hand: A bridge hand with even distribution of cards throughout the suits.

Balancing seat: The position of fourth seat when your LHO opens the bidding followed by two passes.

Blackwood convention: A 4NT artificial bid asking for the number of Aces and Kings.

Convention: A partnership agreement giving a different meaning to a specific bid.

Cover: A play of covering an opponent's honor with your honor to set-up a lower honor in your hand or partner's hand.

Danger hand: A defender gaining the lead can harm the contract.

Finesse: The finesse is a form of declarer play attempting to capture an opponent's honor with lower honor cards. When you finesse you play one defender for a certain card holding.

Fit: The partnership looks for an "Ideal Fit" of 8+cards in any one suit.

Forcing: A bid that forces partner to bid for at least one more round of bidding.

Gerber: A jump to 4♣, an artificial bid as an Ace and King asking convention. Usually used after a 1NT or 2NT opening bid.

Invitational bid: A bid that invites partner to bid again, usually to game level.

Jacoby transfers: An artificial bid by responder of the suit directly below a major suit to show a 5+card major suit when partner opens 1NT or 2NT.

Jump bid: A bid that jumps the bidding one or more levels.

Jump shift: A bid that jumps a level of bidding, and shifts to another suit in the jump bid.

Loser: A card that will lose a trick to the opponents.

Negative double: A bid by responder similar to a takeout double by responder after partner opens a suit that is overcalled by responder's RHO.

Overcall: A bid made over an opponent's bid.

Part score: Contracts below game levels.

Penalty: Points assigned to the defending team when a contract fails.

Preemptive bids: Bids opened at the two, three, four or five-level to show long suits, and hands with 6-10 HCP. The suit should contain two of the top three honors, or three of the top five honors including the 10.

Quantitative bids: A 4NT balanced hand bid following a 1NT opening bid. The 4NT bid asks partner to bid 6NT with 17 points, or pass with 15-16 points. With 17 points, responder can jump to the 6NT slam directly.

Rebid: The subsequent bids by opener or responder.

Re-evaluation: Adding points to your hand due to information gained in the bidding.

Reverse: An opening bid followed by a rebid in a suit higher ranking than first bid suit, and made at the two-level. Shows 17+points, and the first bid suit longer than the rebid suit.

Ruff: Use to a trump card to win a trick when void in the suit led.

Ruff and sluff: The ability to trump or ruff a card in either the declarer or dummy hand, and sluff a losing card in the other hand. Both hands must be void in the suit led.

Sequence: Two or more contiguous cards in a suit.

Set: Defeating the contract.

Singleton: Holding only one card in a suit.

Spot Card: All cards below non-honor cards in a suit.

Stayman convention: An artificial 2♣ bid over a 1NT opening bid, or a 3♣ bid over a 2NT opening bid, asking the NT opener to bid a 4-card major.

Strip and endplays: Declarer strips suits in his hand and the dummy, and plays a card which puts a defender on lead. The defender must lead a suit beneficial to declarer.

Support: Includes simple and limit raises and delayed support of partner's suit.

Takeout doubles: A double call of a bid usually by the LHO of an opening bid, asking partner to bid his best suit. Usually on the one-level, and not a penalty double.

Void: Holding no cards in a suit.

Vulnerability: An artificially assigned state of the contract in duplicate and Chicago scoring. There are higher scores for vulnerable successful contracts then non-vulnerable contracts, and penalties are increased for failed vulnerable contracts.

5+CARD MAJOR BIDDING SYSTEM:

High card points (HCP) for honor cards: ACE = 4; KING = 3; QUEEN = 2; JACK = 1;
LENGTH POINTS: COUNT ONE POINT FOR EACH CARD OVER 4 CARDS IN A SUIT.

OPENING BIDS. Open with a good 12+points and five+cards in a major suit.

No 5+card major, open a 3+cards minor; Open 1♦ with 4♦; open 1♣ with 3-3 minor cards.

JUMP SHIFTS: Opener's jump shift shows 19-21 points and is forcing to game.

RESPONDER'S OPTIONS *WITH* SUPPORT FOR PARTNER'S SUIT.

OPTION #1: (6-10) points: SIMPLE RAISE Three+cards in partner's suit – bid at two-level .
OPTION #2: (10-12) points: LIMIT RAISE Three +cards in partner's suit – jump to three-level.
OPTION #3: 11-15 points: Bid new suit at one or two-level, then with 13-16 points, bid game in partner's suit after partner's non-jump rebid.
OPTION #4: 16+points: Maker a forcing bid and explore for slam.

RESPONDER'S OPTIONS *WITHOUT* SUPPORT FOR PARTNER'S SUIT.

OPTION #5: 6-11 points: A PH responder bids a new suit or notrump at one-level. 10-11 points bids a 5+ heart suit over a 1♠ or any two-level 4+card minor. Responder's jump rebid in his suit shows six+suit, 11-12 points, invite.
OPTION #6: 6+points: A NPH responder's one-level bid of new suit is forcing, non-forcing by PH.
OPTION #7: 10-15 points: Bid new five+card heart suit or any four+card minor suit at the two-level, then jump in your suit with six+cards and 11-12 points, invitational. Non forcing by PH.
OPTION #8: 16+ points: May jump shift on your rebid. Slam invitational.

RESPONDER'S OPTIONS WHEN PARTNER OPENS A MINOR SUIT.

OPTION #9: 6+points: Over opener's minor opening, bid four-card majors up the line.
With no 4+card major, and 5+cards in opener's minor, responder can raise suit to the two-level,
or limit raise to the three-level. NPH forcing or PH non-forcing.

RESPONDER'S NOTRUMP BIDS: BALANCED HANDS – NO SUPPORT

OPTION #10: 6-10 POINTS BID 1NT; 11-12 POINTS BID 2NT; 13-15 POINTS BID 3NT

REBIDS BY OPENER AND RESPONDER: (spades sample suit).

Opener's Raise of Responder's Suit:

	OPENER	RESPONDER	OPENER
12 - 15 POINTS: LOW	1♠	2♠	PASS
16 - 18 POINTS: MEDIUM	1♠	2♠	3♠ INVITE GAME
19 - 21 POINTS: MAXIMUM	1♠	2♠	4♠ BID GAME

Responder's Raise of Opener's Suit:

	OPENER	RESPONDER	
6 - 10 POINTS: LOW	1♠	2♠	SIMPLE RAISE
10 - 12 POINTS: MEDIUM	1♠	3♠	JUMP TO THREE-LEVEL: LIMIT RAISE
13 - 16 POINTS: HIGH	1♠	BID NEW SUIT TWO-LEVEL, THEN BID GAME IN PARTNER'S SUIT AFTER NON-JUMP REBID BY PARTNER.	
17+POINTS: HIGHEST		MAKE A FORCING BID AND EXPLORE FOR SLAM.	

Opener's Raise of Responder's Suit – Four+cards in suit.

12 - 15 POINTS: RAISE RESPONDER'S NEW SUIT TO THE NEXT LEVEL.
16 - 18 POINTS: JUMP IN RESPONDER'S NEW SUIT.
19 - 21 POINTS: JUMP IN RESPONDER'S NEW SUIT TO THE FOUR-LEVEL OR GAME IN A MAJOR .

OPENER'S JUMP SHIFT SHOWS 19-21 POINTS AND IS FORCING TO GAME.

PREEMPTIVE BIDS: NO MORE THAN 10 HCP WITH TWO OF THE TOP THREE HONORS OR
THREE OF TOP FIVE HONORS INCLUDING THE 10. WEAK TWO = SIX-CARD SUIT;
WEAK THREE = SEVEN- CARD SUIT; WEAK FOUR = EIGHT-CARD SUIT, ETC. Responder: Bid game with
15+points or four quick tricks. Bid 2NT asking for outside feature of an ACE OR KING. A new suit by responder is
forcing (partnership agreement). Raise only non-forcing (RONF).

OVERCALLS: Must have good 5+card suit to overcall one or two-level.

8-16 points: One-level overcalls.

12-16 points: Two-level overcalls.

ORDINARY TAKE OUT DOUBLES: 12-16 POINTS - SHORT IN RHO SUIT.

RESPONDER: FORCED TO BID WHEN RHO PASSES.

Forcing bids: 0-8 points- bid one-level; 9-11 points- jump level; 12+ points: cue bid LHO'S SUIT.

BIG HAND TAKOUT DOUBLE: 17+ POINTS

Doubler rebids a new suit, jumps in partner's suit, or jump-shifts into a new suit.

NEGATIVE DOUBLES: PARTNER OPENS, YOUR RHO OVERCALLS:

1♥/1♠ - DOUBLE - NEGATIVE DOUBLE SHOWS BOTH MINOR SUITS;

1♥/2♣ - DOUBLE – NEGATIVE DOUBLE SHOWS SPADES

1♠/2♦ - DOUBLE – NEGATIVE DOUBLE SHOWS HEARTS

RESPONDER MUST HAVE 10+POINTS & FIVE+ CARDS TO BID NEW SUIT AT TWO-LEVEL

NOTRUMP OPENING: 15-17 HCP AND LENGTH POINTS.

NO SINGLETONS - NO VOIDS - ONLY ONE DOUBLETON

OPENER	DISTRIBUTION	POINTS
1 NT	BALANCED HAND - NO VOIDS NO SINGLETONS ONLY ONE DOUBLETON	15-17
RESPONDER	STAYMAN 4-CARD MAJOR	8+
2 NT	NO 4-CARD MAJOR INVITATIONAL TO 3NT	9
3 NT	BID GAME	10-14
4 NT 6 NT	QUANTITATIVE INVITATIONAL BID BID SLAM – BALANCED HAND	15 -16 17-18

STAYMAN RESPONSE TO OPENING 1NT AND 2NT:

2♣/3♣ ARTIFICIAL BID BY RESPONDER ASKS OPENER FOR A FOUR-CARD MAJOR.

OPENER BIDS FOUR-CARD MAJORS UP THE LINE WITH BOTH MAJORS.

2♦. OPENER BIDS 2♦ WITH NO FOUR-CARD MAJOR.

RESPONDER REBIDS OVER 1NT OPENER:

8-9 points: BID 2NT WITH NO FIT IN THE OPENER'S MAJOR

10-14 points: BID 3NT WITH NO FIT IN THE MAJOR

8-9 points: BID 3 OF THE MAJOR WITH A FIT IN OPENER'S MAJOR

10-14 points: BID GAME WITH A FIT IN THE MAJOR

JACOBY TRANSFERS ((TR): RESPONDER BIDS SUIT BELOW HIS FIVE+CARD MAJOR.

RESPONDER BIDS: 2♥ TR TO 2♠; 2♦ TR TO 2♥; OPENER MUST ACCEPT TRANSFER!

RESPONDER REBIDS: Pass with 0-7 points; bid 2NT with 8-9 points; 3NT with 10-14 points.

OPENER REBIDS: 17 points: Accept invitational bids to four of the major or 3NT.

SUPER ACCEPT OF THE TRANSFER: OPENER JUMPS TO THREE OF THE MAJOR

WITH 17 POINTS AND FOUR-CARDS IN THE TRANSFERRD MAJOR SUIT.

SLAM REQUIREMENTS: ARTIFICAL 2♣ OPENER

2♣ - 22+ POINTS OR 8 1/2 PLAYING TRICKS

2♦ - ARTIFICAL - RESPONDER BIDS A WAITING BID.

20-21 POINTS – OPENER BIDS 2NT WITH BALANCED DISTRIBUTION;

RESPONDER CAN BID STAYMAN OR JACOBY TRANSFERS OR 3NT

WHEN YOU HAVE ALL FOUR ACES, 5NT ASKS FOR KINGS

BLACKWOOD CONVENTION - 4NT ASKS FOR ACES AND KINGS.

5♣ - 0 or four aces		6♣ - 0 or 4 kings	
5♦ - 1 ace		6♦ - 1 king	
5♥ - 2 aces		6♥ - 2 kings	
5♠ - 3 aces		6♠ - 3 kings	